WISHES and WEEDS

Gifts from the Wildflower Meadow

By

Carole Rose Dowhan

HARVEST MOON
PUBLISHING

Contents

Contents

May you notice your wildflowers

along the roadside

while traveling to new places.

May you be startled by their beauty

while getting lost in nature.

May you breathe them in your being,

plant them in your soul

and wish upon them with every beat

of your precious,

well-worn heart.

Dedication

For Mark, Mark, and Nick

My wishes come true.

Introduction

Dear Reader,

I am grateful this book has found its way into your hands. My wish is that it finds its way into your heart –the heart that's big enough to hold enormous amounts of love, yet intimate enough for the tiny, secret chambers that cradle your truest self.

This book was designed to be opened to any random page, when you feel disconnected, directionless, and in need of finding meaning in the ordinary. It is my prayer that no matter where you land, you'll discover and connect to your own inner beauty and magic. Like a wildflower, you are rooted to this earth. You continue to grow despite the conditions of your life, evolve through all the phases and learn with every lesson of your life. You are loved and cherished by those who see you as a flower. You are forsaken and abandoned by those who see you as a weed. All the while, you carry a magnificent box of "wild" inside the caverns of your heart. It is filled with extraordinary things meant to be shared. When you find these gifts, your life will take on new meaning. The uncertainty of your reason for being alive will be replaced by a deep knowing in your bones of your purpose. The grey colors that took root from sadness will be replaced by bright, beautiful hues of joy.

What are your wildflower gifts? How do you identify them? How do you claim them? Look to the things that drown out the noise and chaos of living and deliver sweet silence and peace. Look to the things that fill you with intense passion and stop your sorrow from robbing your joy. Look to the things that restore your hope and dismantle your despair. Look to the things that bring you to your knees in gratitude and cause you to fall hopelessly, helplessly and madly in love with the beating of your own heart.

This book is an invitation to view yourself as a precious wildflower – capable of growing against all odds, without external praise or validation and despite endured hardships. Be strong in the face of storms. Tear down the walls you have built for protection that keep you closed off and frightened. Visit the scary places that exist hidden in the dark corners of your soul and bathe them with your brilliant light, until they lose their power. Search for your buried dreams and spend time cultivating them so that your inner beauty can blossom and surpass your outer beauty. Use the garden tools you've gathered from your life lessons to help shatter the image of what you think your life should look like, so that you can begin to live the life meant for you.

You belong to the earth, just as the wildflowers that burst through the soil belong. And like the wildflowers, your time is precious and finite. Be brave. Be bold. Be determined. Search for your gifts. Claim your gifts. Pour the sweetness of your gifts onto the waiting world before it is too late.

May these pages awaken your soul and nourish your spirit.

Go find your wildflowers.
Go find them… now

Peace and Love,
Carole Rose

Believe

Believe

"Born for success he seemed, with grace to win, with heart to hold, with shining fits that took all eyes."
~ Ralph Waldo Emerson

The Night Blooming Cereus is a flowering cactus that only blooms at night. The species of Selenicereus grandiflores, blooms once a year, on one hallowed and holy night, with the darkness of the desert. It releases the beauty it shelters in its own time, on its own terms. Still, it releases what it must release.

There are things living inside you, aching, waiting, scream-ing for release. If you do not believe in your capabilities, your specialness, your worthiness - you cannot hear your gifts calling out and begging to be set free. Inside you lives a poet, a prophet, a teacher, a dancer, a camper, a dreamer, a comedian, a writer, a hero, a lover of life.

2

You may deny your own gifts, believing only others are gifted. You may believe that accomplishments, titles, and fame equate to worth. You may see others on pretty pedestals and feel awestruck of their accomplishments. And you may not yet believe that you are in possession of such magical talent. Much of your energy may have been expended reaching for things, trying to extract stars from the sky, spinning your wheels to survive. But enormous wonders are alive inside you, and your job is to find and share them. You are amazing and rare, with gifts and talents you alone possess. Believe this. Know this. Share this. Once you believe in your specialness you will hear the calling that can no longer be ignored. You are the stuff of stardust and moonbeams, rays of golden sunshine. You are every person you've ever loved, met, brushed shoulders with, admired from afar, or wished you could emulate. You are everything and everywhere.

Do not leave this planet before you believe in the power of your precious gifts. Store them beneath the surface of your soul. Tend to them. Do everything in your power to set them free. Then let them erupt in the stillness of the dark, like the Night Blooming Cereus. Let them greet the sunlight and waken you from slumber. Know that you are free to share your heart, without shackles, barricades, or barbed wire.

3

Begin to view the ordinary as sacred. Allow the light of day and the dark of night to live inside you, for both will give you strength and courage. This is your time. Gather your gifts, burst through the waiting and welcoming soil... and bloom.

Believe in your gifts and give your dreams permission to come true. Become every blessed thing your wishing heart desires. Lead with passion and purpose. Magic happens – when you believe.

Magic

"The appearance of things changes according to the emotions; and thus we see magic and beauty in them, while the magic and beauty are really in ourselves."
~ Kahlil Gibran

Vervain, also known as holy herb or simpler's joy, looks like a magic wand, adorned with bright blue flowers. It was used by early Christians to sprinkle holy water and as medicine to dress wounds. It's used today as an herbal supplement in teas as a natural calming agent.

This wildflower symbolizes magic and calls for the resurrection of all that is enchanting and mystical inside you. There is a deep well of holy herb, sprouting bright blue flowers that fuel your imagination and keep the wonder of youth alive within. Each passing year lived and each stretch of road traveled comes with the risk of losing magic. What is gained in the category of life experience is sometimes lost in the category of life awe. Remain steadfast in your promise to protect the parts of you steeped in wonder, the parts of you that imagine carrying out glorious deeds, the parts of you that keep you light-hearted, childlike and wild.

When you are young, magic is at your disposal. You wish. You dream. You imagine. You wonder. You fantasize. You believe. And because you believe, you perform magic tricks with ease and self-assurance. As you grow up, the magic may seem to vanish because you looked the other way, because you were tending to your grownup problems, because your worries got the best of you, because...you stopped believing.

Never deny the existence of magnificence and magic. Never stop looking for the extraordinary in all things. Throughout life, you will encounter many challenges. Face them with courage. Move past them with determination. Never stop believing in your divinity. Never allow it to be diminished or stolen by nonbelievers. It is your duty to search for your magic. Keep it alive. Release it into the world. Not just this world, where you are bound – walking miles on roads meant for you and walking miles on roads you have no business traveling on. But into other worlds, too, worlds where your dreams are capable of taking flight, where the million things you couldn't say because they caught in your throat are carried by gentle breezes that caress the faces of cherished lost loves. Worlds that hold the answers you seek, the peace you crave, the happiness you chase, and the love that heals a thousand splintered souls.

You are magic. Find it. Protect it. Release it. Live it.

Bare Earth

"Be humble for you are made of earth. Be noble
for you are made of stars."
~ Serbian proverb

Bare earth is the foundation for your wildflowers to emerge.
When soil is free from weeds and grasses, wildflowers flour-
ish. Think blank slate. Think empty canvas.

Bare earth is needed for you to find yourself. Know yourself. Accept yourself. Love yourself. Emptiness gives way to
fullness. Void gives way to filling in. Cracks let in light rays.
There are places inside you aching for release. Let your
vibrant colors surface, your glittering soul emerge, your
bursting heart sing. Start by emptying out the clutter that
hinders your search. Start with the vast nothingness. Start
with bare earth. Start there. Always there.

Cultivate your gifts. Find the places inside where unhealthy weeds took root and attempted to strangle your individuality, your creativity, and your uniqueness. Draw upon the lessons you've learned and allow them to magnify your virtues, enrich the quality of your days, and enable you to evolve into the magnificent being you are meant to be. Find what nourishes you, nurtures your whimsy, and calls forth your magic.

Believe in the process of your journey. Have faith that you can achieve beyond what you know to be possible. You and you alone are responsible for choosing the path you travel. Tear down the walls you have built, the ones you believed kept you safe from hurt and harm. They have become too high, too thick, too impenetrable; the sunlight meant to warm your soul cannot reach you or light you up. Gravitate toward people who lift you higher and allow you to love harder and truer. Question the roads you choose to take. Move among healthy, holy things that raise your reverence for life and cause you to surrender – to the miracles inside you and the awe surrounding you.

Begin on bare earth.

Empty yourself of all that weighs you down. Remove the unnecessary. Begin anew with bare earth and allow your wildflower ways to grow and flourish. Celebrate the beautiful, bare earth that you walk upon.

Bridges

"Love is the bridge between you and everything."
~ Rumi

In the wild, bridges are formed naturally over time, usually by flowing water eroding rock. Fireweed, a tall plant with leaves that change to glowing orange-red, in the fall, can be found growing near the streams and rivers of natural bridges.

Wildflowers serve as bridges that connect you to nature and the source of all creation. Connecting to nature provides a path to your sacred self and allows a deep communing that leads to the birth of peace within. Wildflowers serve as a connecting force capable of silencing the distracting external noise of the world and providing access to all that is hallowed and holy inside.

Bridges connect. The ability to be a bridge of connection with others is a gift to be celebrated. A chain of goodness is made stronger and more resilient when the links are fused. Disconnection among souls leads to weakness and isolation. If you are able to connect people who would otherwise never come together, you are able to heal. Power comes from connectedness and the world becomes greater and holier when love is linked.

Bridges are also symbolic of transitions. Crossing a bridge signifies closing the gap between your present and future selves. In life, you will face many obstacles and challenges. With an open mind, a steady heart, and a desire to overcome difficulty, you can embark on a spiritual transformation that will enable you to experience a deeper love with the divine. The more bridges you cross, the more wisdom you absorb and the stronger you become. Before you cross the threshold to a new perspective, a new way of being and a new life, you need to shed the old things you carry that no longer serve you. Bridges have weight capacities and cannot be crossed while still lugging around heavy burdens and outdated beliefs. Lighten your load. Shed insecurities, narrow-mindedness, and feelings of unworthiness, just as you would remove heavy, cumbersome clothing on a warm summer day.

Cross bridges that lead you to your best self. Keep the things that ignite passion in your heart. Lose the things that extinguish your bliss. Leave your ordinary in order to find your wild. Search for the internal things that are saturated with your true identity – things that make you daring and extraordinary. Hold tightly to the rare parts of you that are utterly irreplaceable because only you are in possession of them. Hold tightly to the beliefs that cause passion to bubble up and move you to do great things in the world. You cannot be duplicated. You are an original creation in this boundless universe.

Cross bridges that place you on the path of deeper connection with your sacred self. Before you cross them, lose the things that weigh you down. Lose your ordinary. Find your wild. When you feel anxious and uncertain about crossing a bridge, find comfort in knowing that on the other side of today – is a tomorrow filled with gifts meant for you to find, people meant for you to love, and life meant for you to live.

Candytuft

"I have dreamed in my life, dreams that have stayed with me
ever after, and changed my ideas; they have gone through
and through me, like wine through water,
and altered the color of my mind."
~ Emily Bronte

*Candytuft, also known as Iberis, is a perennial wildflower.
It can grow twelve to eighteen inches tall, with shiny, green
leaves and flowers that grow in clusters of white, with red
or pink or purple hues. Each flower contains four petals and
gives off a sweet fragrance with a cotton candy-like appearance.
It has properties said to relieve rheumatism and arthritis.*

Even though this blossom brings beauty to the meadows
that it graces, the meaning attached to this dreamy wildflower is indifference. Allowing indifference to take root in

your wildflower life is akin to inviting and ignoring a weed that has the potential to overpower, overgrow and strangle your passions. Searching for meaning and truth in everyday living requires having a core set of beliefs and convictions that you adhere to and live by. Indifference is deadly.

Cotton-candy dreaming is required to breathe magic into the creative parts of your soul and to lay the groundwork for your wishes to catch air, fly high, and become reality. However, remaining in that dreamy state can render you neutral or numb, and that doesn't bode well for a seeker of passion. Make certain that you are clear about your convictions – the truths that resonate within you and bubble up with fervor. Make certain that you do not become numb by difficulties. Gather wisdom and strength through experience and include them in your arsenal of garden tools, so that you may weed out the unnecessary things that dull your shine and dim your light.

Whatever you believe and whatever you are, bring to these your fire and fury. If you are happy, laugh. If you are sad, cry. If you are angry, scream. But if you are indifferent, fight like hell to wake up and snap out of a poisonous place that has the potential to paralyze. Make certain that your laughter leads to the purity of joy and is not acting as plaster to cover up painful parts. With every fiber inside you, allow your sadness to burst forth and greet the light of day. Allow your joy to reach deep into your bones and relieve the ache that resides there. Allow your anger to spur you to take action and transform. Whatever is inside of you deserves to be set free.

Do not allow indifference to take root. Do not bury your candytuft seeds. Keep the whimsy. Keep the glory. Keep the conviction. Let these grow and bloom inside you, so that the grey colors will never seep into your soul and erase your lovely colors.

Wisteria

"One word frees us of all the weight and pain of life.
That word is love."
~ Sophocles

Wisteria is a deciduous, woody vine that belongs to the pea
family. It can be found growing wild, near forests or any
place that has fertile, well-drained soil. It prefers sunny
conditions to thrive. It blooms in spring and summer and
produces white, pink, purple or blue flowers. Some wisteria
may give off the fragrance of grapes and the smell is said to
attract many bees and hummingbirds that aid in the pollination process. Wisteria possesses magnificent beauty, as
its winding flowers lay in clusters that seem to bow their
weeping heads in sorrow and with an heir of reverence. The
symbolic meaning of this beautiful bloom represents sadness over lost love but also of the overwhelming strength

that the heart possesses to endure mistreatment and over-come hardship.

Hardships, challenges, and difficulty enter your life when you least expect them. Things may be running smoothly; you finally feel as though you are managing to move past the perils placed in your path so you can merrily meet your miracles. And suddenly, you are struck with circumstances that thrust you into upheaval and distress. Hard times enter your life in the forms of illness, loss and heartbreak. And although each of these things has the ability to level you, they may also present an opportunity to elevate you.

Dealing with difficulty forces you to hold on and let go, simultaneously. It's a very difficult and tricky thing to adapt to. But mastering this task is paramount to the rhythm of your life. Each time you embark on a challenge, you will learn what to hold onto and what to let go of. You will become better at relishing the sacred moments of your life while accepting the hard times and seeking to move past them. You will become better at holding onto faith and letting go of cynicism. You will become better at holding onto sweetness and letting go of bitterness. You will become better at holding onto love and letting go of hate.

The earth on which you walk, tethered to a body equipped with mind, heart, and soul, is not a place to live without spiritual connection and deep-rooted faith. Dealing with anything that brings you to your knees in desperation is easier when you believe both in yourself and in a higher power. Clinging tightly to your faith will embolden you to anything life throws your way. Surrendering to a power greater and holier will keep you safe and strong and sur-viving, until the darkness passes.

Never give up. Believe that the most painful times will lead to your most joyful moments. Believe that your darkest hours hold the power to shine the brightest light on your meadow. Believe that your worst heartbreak sets the foundation for growing a heart stronger and more capable of holding enormous love.

You are strong and resilient. You are a true survivor. When life gets unbearably difficult, let go of your self-im-portance and the belief that you hold all the power. Bow your head in reverence to your maker, just as the wisteria bows down its enchanting fragrant blossoms and trust that you are surrendering to your truest transformation and sweetest salvation.

Surrender

"The best things in life are nearest; Breath in your nostrils, light in your eyes, flowers at your feet, duties at your hand, the path of right just before you."
~ Robert Louis Stevenson

Baby's breath, or Gypsophilia, is also known as soaproot or chalk plant. There are approximately thirty-five species that belong to this group of perennial or annual plants. Some grow bushy and up to two feet tall, while others grow low to the ground. They prefer full or partial sun and moist soil. They bear dainty white or pink flowers that branch out from long, slender stems. The stems can be easily separated and the flowers can be dried and used in bouquets or gardens to fill in the empty spaces.

Baby's breath can serve to remind you of the fee ing of empty spaces that exist within you and the overwhelming need you will struggle with to fill those spaces. Wildflowers are temporary inhabitants of this world. You share this truth with them. Your time is limited. Spend it wisely. Filling yourself with inconsequential things that don't matter is a waste of your precious time. Everything that you need to live an authentic, worthwhile life is already inside you. Instead of attempting to reach for things to ease the empty feeling you have, search for and claim the glorious riches that you have been given.

Surrender yourself to the breath of God that surrounds you and allow your empty spaces to be filled and your soul to be healed. You are beauty, surrounded by a climate that may fail to reflect your beauty. Things are not always how you wish them to be. Things change. People change. Loved ones grow older, wearier, ill. The ones you love the most, may lose their health, their ability to move, their memory. Heartache ensues and sets the stage for cracks to form. These grow wider and deeper with every hardship. Allow the breath of God to enter you and to fill in those empty spaces before they grow into chasms and leave you walking through the world riddled with holes.

Never believe you are facing this journey alone. Notice the signs surrounding you, those sent from another world. They will provide you with clues for dealing with your struggles. Breathe in the breath of God. It will provide you with sustenance and give you strength to carry on.

Look for the bursts of special that go unnoticed by most and conjure up precious memories...a smile from a passing stranger that resembles a smile of an old cherished friend, a flower that bursts through a sidewalk crack and deepens your love of nature, a sunset with colors that call to mind the iced-sherbet your mother gave you as a child on a hot summer day, how it melted in rainbow rivers down your ice-cream cone and onto your hands.

Allow kindness to soften your sharp edges and allow you to meld with all creation. God's grace is ever present. Keep faith at the forefront of your wildflower meadow. Nourish it. Tend to it. Draw strength from it.

Surrender to the simple moments held within each day. Be open to them. Search for them. Count them among your blessings. Surrender to God and allow his love to fill you up and help you carry on.

Lotus Blooms

"Without mud, you cannot have a lotus flower. Without suffering, you have no ways in order to learn how to be understanding and compassionate. Happiness is the lotus flower, and the suffering is the mud. So the practice is how to make use of the suffering, make use of the mud, to create the flower, the happiness, and this is possible."

~ Thich Nhat Hanh

The lotus flower symbolizes serenity, purity, beauty, and grace. It grows in muddy water. Its white or pink petals are shaped like daggers. Its leaves are paddle-shaped and some lie above the water, bringing a buoyancy to the plant. The flower opens with the rising sun and closes with the rising moon. The fragrance emitted from the bloom is said to be intoxicating.

The lotus is considered to be sacred and many life lessons can be gleaned from this flower. The stages of growing represent stages of growth, self-awareness, and enlightenment. The mud from which it emerges signifies the great suffering of life that all humans endure in different stages of intensity and throughout various stages of growth. Being in the mud isn't a desirable place to dwell, but it can be a place of deep reflection needed to reign in your gifts, set your life course, and get right with yourself.

Mud molds. Mud softens. Mud transforms. It sets conditions for your Maker to mold you upon his potter's wheel and sculpt you into the person capable of facing your future. Above the mud there is rigidity, a hardening of self that takes place. Your future self needs to be shaped in order to prepare you to en-dure hardships that lie ahead, and to open you up to absorbing and reveling in the blessings and delights that await you.

Being immersed in mud delivers deep teachings. The body you carry forward once difficulty passes is branded with a knowing that sears your very soul. Hold tightly to that truth when in the mess and the muck. Know that inhabiting this sacred space is where growth takes root. Once released from the hardship, your eyes will have learned to focus on the identity of those that enter your life. There will be a clear delineation of whom you're meant to move toward and whom you're meant to leave behind.

Embrace the magic and the mystery of the muddy waters. Hold tightly to your faith. Surrender to your lessons. Allow yourself to be shaped and transformed. Open up to the renewal of spirit and awakening of your soul. Know that beautiful things rise from difficulty. Be washed clean and like the lotus, open your consecrated petals one by one and allow life to unfold and blossom.

Allow suffering to soften, not harden you, so that you can emerge as a better soul, live a more harmonious life, and reach new levels of awareness. If you recognize a kindred spirit weighed down in the suffering of muddy waters, counsel them, console them and help them see that through this experience they will become more of who they are meant to be.

Living in the Center

"Give all to love; obey thy heart."
~ Ralph Waldo Emerson

Queen Anne's Lace is also known as bird's nest, due to the fact that the flower head dries after it dies and resembles a nest-like shape. Seen as an invasive weed by many, it grows in dry fields and along sunny roadsides, reaching its peak in the midsummer months. It has a strong scent that lures a multitude of insects to feast on its blossoms. The plant consists of a single stem that can hold hundreds of round clustered, white flowers that resemble lace. At the center of the lace bundle lies a single, purple dot. Legend claims that the dot signifies a finger prick from Queen Anne of England, who had an affinity for lace on her dresses.

To behold this controversial wildflower that represents sanctuary and protection, one is reminded that life is lived mainly on the periphery, where the multitude of clustered flowers reside: those lacy places where you'll spend most of your time, performing tasks that need to be completed and bustling about with the business of living. There are millions of ways to spend your time, entertain yourself, and align yourself safely with shallow, surface living. But it takes courage to visit and live from the center, purple dot portion of your life, the part where blood is spilled, where imperfection reigns, and where broken pieces of you lay scattered about.

Living your life from your center is how you will become acquainted with your deepest self, the one who isn't always put together, doesn't always have answers, isn't always fulfilled or self-assured… but is most definitely always real. Don't allow yourself to play it safe by living on the periphery of your life. Don't cheat yourself out of the gift of knowing your truest self. See the outer, lacey places as the universe. See the center, purple dot as your heart and live from that hallowed place.

You hold a coveted spot in the vastness of creation. An all-knowing, all-powerful being fell so in love with the idea of you, that you were created. Sit with that concept. Allow it to sink into your consciousness. You were uniquely designed with the intention that you have something valuable to be shared with those that you meet. Live from your center. Be brave. Be bold.

Dig deep. Dive into the core, the very heart of your identity. Visit the part of you that offers sanctuary to your soul. Get to know your innermost self and all the astonishing qualities you possess.

You are valuable to this world. You are irreplaceable. You are unique. Blood was spilled so that you could be the purple dot in the center of a lacy, "miracle flower universe" and hold a special place in the landscape of the "center of God's heart."

Wishing on Wildflowers

*"If you wish to see the valleys, climb to the mountain top; if you
desire to see the mountain top; rise into the cloud; but if you
seek to understand the cloud, close your eyes and think."*
~ Kahlil Gibran

All the beauty that you notice, covet, and embrace in this
world is planted inside you, where it grows, spills onto others, and accompanies you from this world to the next. Absorb
every precious ounce of awe that you encounter. Look to the
ground for things that stir your soul and cause you to kiss the
earth in gratitude. Look to the sky for things that swell your
heart and cause you to fall to your knees in surrender.

Wish on everything: the miniscule mushroom that sprouted
and may have come from woodland fairies, the butterfly that

brushed so close to your face that you swore it was a sign from the other side. Wish on the shiny penny lying on the ground while you walked your children to the bus stop. Wish on candles and coins and blades of fresh, green grass. Wish on the days gone by that make you ache with longing. Wish on the days yet to be that whisper a promise of peace.

Wish on the day that lies before you as it cradles you with out-stretched arms and fills you with a knowing that you will make a difference in this world. You will triumph before the stars that you wished on, blanket the dark sky and allow slumber to reach your weary bones and burned-out body.

Wish on wildflowers, the ones that burn inside, churn passion, ignite creativity, and light you up. For just as you look up toward the heavens for bright things to wish upon, there are glorious, winged creatures looking down on a dark and some-times bitter earth. They are wishing, too. The more beauty you amass, the brighter you shine, and the more brilliant you appear, the greater the chances for their wish of comfort to overthrow despair, their wish of hope to overthrow fear, their wish of love to overthrow hate.

Absorb beauty that surrounds you. Wish on wildflowers. And shine brightly in thoughts and deeds, so that heaven, can wish... on you.

Grow

Spring Beauty Maps

"To map out a course of action and follow it to
an end requires courage."
~ Ralph Waldo Emerson

"Spring Beauty" is one of the earliest wildflowers to blanket
floors of forests and transform them into enchanted places. The
tiny blooms consist of light and dark pink-hued petals. Lines are
etched into the delicate petals and serve as road maps for bees in
search of decadent, sweet nectar.

You possess lines or marks etched onto your soul. These soul
markings hold clues to the direction meant for you to travel,
the tasks meant for you to perform, the people meant for you
to meet. When you are on the course meant for you, follow-

ing your map, your choices, and your daily works fill you with moments of overwhelming joy and wholeness. Cultivate these places inside you that store your gifts. Educate yourself about what you are capable of contributing to others. Embrace your individuality, your creativeness, and your uniqueness. Use everything you've learned to magnify your worthwhile virtues, the ones that enrich your days and allow you to evolve into the magnificent being you are meant to become.

Be diligent and deliberate about finding what nourishes you, what nurtures your whimsy and calls forth your own particular brand of magic. These discoveries help you to journey beyond what you believe possible and to achieve what appears to be impossible. In order to follow the maps meant for you, you will be called on to tear down internal walls. You've been building them forever. You believed they could shield you from hurt and harm. And every time you suffered heartache or disappointment, you continued their construction, until you became a master wall builder. But the walls you have built have become too high, too thick, too impenetrable. It's difficult to read your internal maps in the dark. Allow the light to reach your heart and to illuminate the paths that will provide you with lessons you need most – those that will enable you to seek out your truth, find your purpose, and move in the direction of your glorious destiny.

Tear down the walls you have built inside. Let the sunlight reach your heart, warm your spirit and help you hone your precious gifts. Trust the map etched upon your soul. It is the direction you are meant to follow in your life. It will guide you in your search for every lesson you are meant to learn, every transformation you are meant to experience and every blessing you are meant to absorb, so that you can live out your true purpose and bask in the spring beauty of the miracle of life.

Cleansing Storms

"When we look deeply into the heart of a flower, we see clouds, sunshine, minerals, time, the earth, and everything else in the cosmos in it. Without the clouds there could be no rain, and without rain there would be no flower."
~ *Thich Nhat Hanh*

Storms reach deep into places where wildflowers grow. The plants stand strong against the blustering wind and the cutting rain. They survive against all odds. They become wildflower warriors.

Just as the storms reach the wildflowers, so too do they reach you. Storms come in the form of heartache, such as when you love another, not knowing they are incapable of love. Storms come in the form of illness and cause you to come face to face with your mortality. Storms come in the form of life changes, the kind that bring you to your knees and force you to reevaluate your purpose. Storms come in the form of loss, causing you to mourn deeply souls that gave meaning to life. You cannot seek shelter when the sky targets you with thundering bursts of fury and rains down liquid agony, or when a person who is hell bent on manipulation targets you, or when people or things that once provided comfort are ripped from your grasp.

The walls, barricades, and reinforcements you've worked so hard to build cannot protect you. Let the storms come. Don't fight them. Let them blow through your life and render you helpless. Let them crack you open, until every blessed part of you spills out onto the cold, wet, barren, ready soil. Let them leave you raw and defenseless. Once you are broken open, you will have a choice to make: Will you put yourself back together with the unhealed pieces of your past – or will you use this blessed opportunity to acknowledge your wounds, learn from your pain, and choose a new path?

When you choose a new way of living, the wounds of the past can be confronted, dealt with, and finally healed. The moment your former self shatters is holy. Exposed hurt, buried pain, and sharp fragments are able to absorb rays of sunlight that bounce off of the forest trees, warm weary bones and ultimately heal. Heavenly raindrops are able to reach your parched spirit and wash you clean. Gusts of powerful wind blow through your soul and make you whole.

Venture outside after a storm. Notice the trees that no longer stand. Once colossal, solid towers that pierced the sky now stand split open; their leaves, branches, and twigs litter the saturated soil. Lightning bolts will enter your life in the form of hardship. Like the mighty trees, you will be split open, your foundation rocked to its core. Pieces of you will be scattered about. You will feel leveled and devastated and hopeless. Th s is the time to cling tightly to a belief in a creator that dwells above the treetops. Have faith that you are never alone. Know that after the storm comes the sun. Allow the warmth of its rays to shine on your brokenness. When you are this exposed and raw, your deepest wounds can no longer hide within. Healing comes with the light. You are a true survivor. You are a true warrior. You are a true wildflower.

Once the healing has taken place and you are restored to a state of grace, take inventory of your life. Know that you are stronger than before the storm, now capable of venturing out of the safety of your protective cocoon. And with the skills of a warrior and someone who has danced in the rainstorm and survived, you can move forward into your future. Look around you and notice those who stayed beside you. They are a part of your loyal band of travelers through life. Those who ran from you and sought cover when your storm came were never meant to stay.

*Let the storms come. Let the raindrops cleanse you. Let the
wind blow through you. Allow your hardened heart to become
softened. Allow your resolve to be strengthened. Allow your
broken pieces to become blessed. Allow passion to be planted
deep within so you can continue your journey – fully awake,
fully intact, and fully alive.*

Bleeding Hearts

"You have to keep breaking your heart until it opens."
~ Rumi

Bleeding Hearts are also called Lady's Locket or Valentine Flowers. They are pink or white, heart-shaped blossoms that dangle gracefully from long, winding stems, surrounded by a bed of lush, green leaves. The tips of the blooms are tinged with what appears a small drop of deep pinkish-red blood.

The bleeding heart wildflower reminds you that your heart is the center of your being. There are those who choose to move through life authentically and wear their heart on their sleeve. There are those who prefer to hide their tenderness in an effort to keep themselves safe from hurt, believing that if they shield themselves with layers of armor, they will remain safe from those who make sport of hurting hearts. Wearing armor may offer protection, but it also blocks the light. Your heart is your truest treasure and it desperately needs the ebb and flow of love in order to sustain its beating. When you deny owning an enormous heart, or attempt to shield it or hide it, you are limiting the amount of love that enters your world.

When love isn't at the center of living, your experience of life is dull and meaningless. The wildflower colors inside you become muted and the passion inside you, dulled. When your heart is closed off to the magic of loving, you are not fully awake, alive, or capable of absorbing the awe that drenches your spirit with the gift of grace. And it is this gift of grace that allows you to see your life for the true miracle that it is.

When you make the decision to live an open-hearted life, you plant miracle seeds of love deep within. You lose the fear that shackles you to a life of darkness and dread. And you align yourself with the lightness of being and the passion of giving. You are, in essence, choosing to become the hero of your own story, because you are living each day from a place of courage and conviction, a more genuine existence for having shed that which no longer serves you. Your heart is now filled with gratitude because you are able to give and receive love. When this awakening inside you occurs and you finally claim your heart and proudly fly your "heart on your sleeve" flag – your life becomes illuminated with all that is sacred.

The fear of being hurt not only paralyzes; it functions as a barrier to beauty. Your heart slowly dies, like petals withering at season's end. But when you do the work required to shed fear, to tear down walls, to care for others with an open heart, you begin to radiate pure love. Living from a place of authenticity and gratitude exposes your heart to every experience that life offers.

Bleeding hearts are a thing of beauty - the one that grows wild. Bleeding hearts are a thing of transformation – the one that beats inside your chest. You cannot save another from the deep pain of a broken, bleeding heart. You are at risk when you open up to another. Let go and share the deepest parts of yourself with those you trust and deem worthy. Experiencing heartbreak cleanses. It clears a path for renewal and growth. After heartaches, you are forever changed and there is sadness in saying goodbye to your former self. But you cannot learn anything new or grow by keeping love out and staying unchanged.

Your heart is the direct line to your soul. It leads to the sacred connection you long for with your creator. One misconception of heartbreak is that you are "less than" because others stole precious pieces of you.

When you offer yourself to another and they turn out to be incapable of reciprocating your love, your heart may be broken but it remains whole. The break clears a path for the birth of a heart that is capable of loving harder and more completely. Trust that the pain that accompanies heartbreak also signifies growth; after the ache subsides, you are left with a bigger heart capable of loving much more truly, fully, and deeply. Wholeheartedly.

Once healed, you will be called on to help other bleeding hearts, for you are now skilled in the lessons of the heart. Be a good steward of this most precious life lesson. When you recognize the painful, familiar cry of the heartbroken, reach out to them, pull them close, and help them climb out of the discarded waste pile where only weeds belong. Remind them of their beauty, their brilliance, and their light. Help them heal and shed their fears. *Get back to dancing with the wildflowers.*

Let the bleeding heart flower remind you that your heart is the source of internal riches and leads to a life with direction, meaning and purpose. Give love. Receive love. Keep your heart open… always.

Milkweed Gifts

"There is a candle in your heart, ready to be kindled. There is a
void in your soul, ready to be filled, You feel it, don't you?"
~ Rumi

Milkweed is a fragrant plant that prefers full sunshine. Pink,
flower clusters that form a sphere, adorn the top of its tall,
sturdy stems. A magical plant that monarch butterflies deem
worthy enough to lay their eggs upon and the resulting cater-
pillar feeds upon its leaves.

You may view the milkweed plant as a pesky weed and want
it gone, or you may choose to allow it to grow and flourish n
your garden. In life, you get to choose what to discard, what
to keep, what is broken, what is blessed, what is a flower, and
what is a weed. People will come and go in your meadow.
Some will hurt your heart and you will want them gone to stop

the pain. It may take years, but you will eventually hold a place of gratitude in your heart for those who left you broken. Being broken-hearted offers a miracle opportunity to witness parts you never knew existed – parts that hold your mystery, your magic and your treasured milkweed gifts.

When you find yourself bent, broken, and discarded, you reside in the holiest of spaces. For it is then that you are seeking healing light. And it is then that you are open to God's grace. Pain is certainly felt, but your senses are awakened to glorious things as well. The sound of nature surrounds you. The chirping birds resemble a heavenly symphony – rich with the promise of eternity. The sound of wind rustling through the trees translates into messages of wisdom from the woods. Inspiration is found in majestic mountains and the way the clouds magically move over their glorious peaks. Being broken-hearted empties you out of all that is heavy and cumbersome. And when you are leveled and emptied out, you stop carrying the things that don't matter and begin to look at life with new eyes, an open heart, and a renewed sense of spirit. You are ready to be filled up with warm, golden rays of sunlight. You are open to being bathed in the glow of moonbeams. The night is no longer a frightening, dark place.

Dust off your dreams. Remember the things that stirred your soul and fed your passion. Gather those things close and allow yourself to grow – beyond what you believed you were capable of. And as you pray for your heart-pain to go away, begin to view yourself as a vessel filled with hope. Just as the milkweed delivers nourishment to flying flowers with gossamer wings, begin to believe that you have much to contribute to the world. Realize that loving yourself is paramount. Allow yourself to enter into a deeper union with the glorious act of living. The grey spaces you held inside that caused you to doubt your worth and made you fearful of the future? These are replaced with rich, healing color.

See yourself as a glorious flower in life's meadow. Deem your place as valuable and worthwhile. While you are on this earth, grow and flourish and give back. Learn your lessons so that you can grow stronger, wiser and more capable.

Live like the milkweed. Allow those close to you to make mistakes, to change, and to grow. Nourish them. Help them heal and move forward. Allow yourself to move past being broken and rebuild your heart with the healed parts that hold and nourish your miracle gifts.

Freedom

"Dance, when you're broken open. Dance, if you've torn the bandage off. Dance in the middle of the fighting. Dance in your blood. Dance when you're perfectly free."

~ Rumi

Indian Paintbrush, also known as Painted Lady or Butterfly Weed, is a member of the figwort family. The leaves on this meadow dweller are long, narrow and pointy. The flowers are clustered, tube-shaped and resemble a paintbrush. The top of the flower holds a bright red color, making it appear to have been dipped in paint. Ancient legend claims a Native American Indian was painting the sunset, left his brushes on the ground and they blossomed into these glorious, well-loved plants.

The color red signifies passion, heart, and emotion. It is said that carrying a few petals of this magical, red-dipped flower in a sachet will release negative energy and attract love. Let this be a reminder that you are a living, breathing paintbrush. You are filled with bright beautiful color and your life is a sacred expression of that. Live each day with passion. The love that flows to and from your heart deepens the colors that saturate your paintbrush body and allows you to paint your life with heavenly hues. Drench the earth with your glorious colors and leave behind a legacy of love that will outlive your time on earth. Paint each day that you are blessed to awaken to with bold, deliberate strokes of wildflower magic.

Grow freely like the blooms of the Indian paintbrush, so that others will gravitate toward your beauty. Paint your days with thick layers of joy, passion, and hope – to heal places you may have grown sad, flat, or faithless. Travel light. Rid yourself of all that weighs you down and causes your colors to become mud-died. Fly away from things that bind you to the perceptions of others and keep you shackled to a life that craves validation. When the darkness appears in the form of unavoidable chal-lenges, don't allow it to stick and cast a somber, murkiness on your inner color palette. Wash yourself clean in the river of light and love. Own your essence by living simply, authentically and unencumbered. When the hard times surface, believe in your ability to persevere.

Be grateful for the colorful gifts your Creator has planted within you. Allow them to surface and work tirelessly to hone and share them. Know that all great things are born inside, where the seeds of love are nurtured and rooted. What springs forth is personal freedom, a state of grace and colorful realized dreams, capable of adding shades of brilliance to an otherwise black-and-white world.

Live life freely and paint each new day with your beauty. Be your most colorful self – the self you were born to be. Do it without the consent of others. Paint boldly. Paint wildly. Paint freely.

Growing Conditions

"Accept the things to which fate binds you and love the people
with whom fate brings you together, but do so with
all your heart."
~ Marcus Aurelius

*Flowers bloom and grow better near those that have comparable
conditions, soil structure, sun requirements and moisture needs.*

Like a flower, you also grow better in proximity to those that
require similar conditions. You don't always have to grow in
the same direction or at the same pace as those near. But you
have to have the freedom to grow next to one another and
you must be certain that others don't attempt to pluck your
freedom from you. You may believe the ones you allow near
share the same heart as you. This prevents you from believing
and identifying others that may carry less than pure intentions.

Remember that you are unique to this world and not everyone who walks this earth is capable of goodness.

When you live compassionately, you possess a special knowing for when others are hurting, and you help them. When you offer your time, comforting words, and pieces of your heart, you help others heal. When you live from a place of giving and helping rather than taking and hurting, from a place of building up rather than tearing down, you enhance the lives of everyone you touch. But living from a place of love also opens a doorway for pretenders of love to enter.

Being a healer of hearts many times attracts broken spirits with sharp, jagged edges capable of inflicting pain if you get too close. Lights that shine attract dwellers of the dark. Know that they will come and know that you risk losing your light if you keep them near.

It takes courage to keep an open heart in a world where many attempt to break your spirit for sport. It hurts like hell when others treat you poorly, betray you, and use you for their own selfish motives. But know that hot tears shed over inflicted hurt burn deep lessons into your well-worn skin. These will protect your heart from future hurt. When someone you've trusted attempts to steal your beautiful wildflower ways, keep your eyes open to their motives. You cannot fix them. You cannot change them. You cannot keep their good and discard their bad. You must uproot them from your life. You must acknowledge that they lack the same growing conditions as you. You must part ways. Do not judge them or assign feelings of resentment or anger toward them. Instead, detach from a place of gratitude, for they have taught you much. Feel fortunate to have crossed paths with them because you have evolved into a stronger, wiser, more whole version of yourself. Pray for their peace, their prosperity, and for a long and happy wildflower life.

Release those who no longer encourage growth in you. Give yourself back to the earth, the sky, and the air, and get back to the business of growing.

Wanderers

---

*"Trees go wandering forth in all directions with every wind,
going and coming like ourselves, traveling with us around the
sun two million miles a day, and through space
heaven knows how fast and far!"*
~ John Muir

There are wildflowers that exist unseen, hidden in deep, damp
forests. Bunchberry, also known as dwarf dogwood, is one of
those elusive and hidden blossoms. It has four white petals that
are perched atop a whirl of leaves, with the actual pale, green
flower, lying on the white petals.

Many wildflowers are hidden away in deep, lush, green forests,
far from the risk of being trampled upon by civilized shoe
wearers. They are waiting patiently for someone to pass by
and discover them. There are things inside you that also wait

patiently to be discovered. The journey to find and unleash the wildness inside you begins with a stirring in your soul. An ache starts to gnaw at you internally. At first, you attempt to ignore it. After all, you have things to do. Real things, solid things, things that have weight to them and things that demonstrate to the world that you are worthy – because you produce. It has taken years of commitment to reach a level of accomplishment. Being goal oriented has brought you much success. And you tackle to do lists like nobody's business. Why would you jeopardize everything that you've worked so hard for to go "find yourself"? Such a foolish cliché that others follow because they don't have a clear path to success. There's no time to go inside with so much to achieve on the outside, you tell yourself.

Still, the ache to grow in ways you don't yet understand grows stronger and stronger until you have no choice but to pay attention. You stop fighting. You get quiet. You start listening. And with an internal knowing, a passion is ignited. You feel alive, as electricity courses through your veins and you are propelled forward, led to a sacred space that has nothing to do with spreadsheets, quotas, or forecasts. This moment is your magical time. It is your time to go inside. It is your time to search for missing things that are hidden in the stillness, in the darkness, in the depths. It is your time to wander, to search, to claim.

Wildflowers are waiting patiently for someone to pass by. They exist unseen. No one speaks of their loveliness. No one tends to them, waters or dotes on them. Yet their beauty is real and raw. They are calling out to be discovered. They long to have their glorious scent mix with another's in-breath. To have their heavenly colors absorbed, to feel the touch of fingers on their delicate, velvety petals.

They are waiting for you – and only you – to pass by. The "you" that is certain of your identity. The "you" that has claimed your uniqueness. The "you" that walks with a deliberate stride, assured of a million, tiny purposes you carry in your soul suitcase of a body. The "you" that has chosen to set out on a gift-searching expedition, armed only with courage and the conviction that the universe needs your particular brand of wildness...to heal.

Be a wanderer. Go find your wildflowers. Find them now.

In-Between

The gardenia is a part of the coffee plant family, 'Rubraceae'. The flowers of the plant grow on small shrubs between early spring and late summer. There are over 142 species of these plants. If water touches the petals of the flower, they turn the color of brown coffee. They possess an extremely strong, pretty, fragrance.

This blossom symbolizes sweetness, a rare virtue in a world filled, at times, with bitterness. There is a place that exists between the sweetness and the bitterness of life. When sorrows and hardships become too hard to bear, you will find yourself straddling this 'In-Between' place. You will feel the sweet and the bitter, simultaneously. You will feel hidden and exposed, invigorated and weary, raw and numb. You will be hiding in the shadows while dancing in the light. The time will come when you must choose.

Stay in this ambiguous place while you must, but do not stay there forever. Believe in the sweetness of life. Accept your hardships with grace and courage. Extract every ounce of beauty from the sorrowful times, from the painful times, from the 'In-Between". Then keep the sweetness alive inside, for it allows you to move through the world on your own terms. Stay true to the natural inclination woven into you at birth, the gift meant for you to spread and protect and never lose to the bitterness.

This is your challenge. Refuse to be absorbed by the darkness. Refuse to turn bitter. Choose instead to recognize those with whom your soul is aligned: the givers, the empathetic feelers, the ones in the trenches who care, who help, who hug with their hearts and shelter with their arms, the ones capable of understanding what others feel. Then, pull them close... and pour out your sweetness on them.

Preserve and protect the quality of your tenderness and the essence of your gentleness. Do not allow yourself to be swallowed up by the bitterness that shows up in your life. Choose, instead to lead with the sweetness you exude. Let it lift you from the in between place and let it triumph over the bitter.

Forgiveness

*The blue violet grows wild in meadows, lawns, and forests
floors. Many see it as a pesky weed, as it possesses deep, dense
roots capable of spreading rapidly. The tiny bloom consists of
two petals on top, two petals situated on the side, and a striped
petal that adorns the bottom and acts as a flag that attracts bees
to the sweet nectar for pollination. Violets are edible, providing
they are not doused in chemicals, and are often used to decorate
fancy culinary confections.*

Violets are tiny, delicate, and beautiful in a simplistic, uncomplicated way. They give off a sweet aroma, especially when the
petals are crushed. Violets are known as the flower of forgive-

ness, hardly something we think of as uncomplicated and simple.

In fact, the act of forgiveness is worlds away from the simplicity of the sweet violet blossom that it represents. Forgiveness does not grow easily along country roadsides or tuck itself away in wild flower fields. It does not have deep roots that adhere to the soil and spread quickly without intervention. And it is not granted easily, no matter how loving or compassionate of a human you believe yourself to be. When someone you've allowed close to your heart betrays you, a deep wound forms with a jumble of intricate layers that are woven tightly together, like a flower bud with petals that refuse to open. The desire to avoid dealing with the dreadful feelings of hurt is overwhelming. And the decision to begin the arduous process of forgiveness cannot be rushed. You must warm up to the idea of granting mercy – slowly, just as the earth thaws from winter's deep freeze. You may desperately want to forgive and move past the pain. But forgiveness comes in its own time.

The deep hurt that caused your shoulders to slump, your eyes to mist over, and your heart to ache takes precious time to unravel. Betrayal comes as hard-driving rain one minute and soft showers the next. But the raindrops continue to fall from the sky and sting as they reach your naked flesh. Stay open to forgiveness. Pray for it. Wish for it with all your heart. But wait for it. Don't hurry it. Don't expend energy attempting to understand the motives or intentions of the one who wounded you. In fact, don't focus on them at all. This storm is between you and you. It's between the "innocent, shocked you" and the "hot, angry you." When you place great energy into focusing on the person who has wounded you, they become your hostage; once they are held captive within the walls of your world, it becomes more difficult to grant them release. And in this way, the personal growth meant for you to reach becomes locked away in a prison constructed of human bones, not iron bars. The longer you hold someone hostage, the more their actions gain power and the more they act as a weed to your wildflower meadow – overpowering, overgrowing, and crowding out the wishes, dreams, and goals you planted for your life.

Forgive by experiencing the hurt hurled your way. You don't have to accept into your life the poison attached to the hurt. The disrespect came from another and by not accepting it into your life, it stays with them and is not absorbed. Once time has passed, soil has been watered with warm tears, and your heart has begun to ache less...forgiveness has arrived. In that holy moment, you have a choice to make. Will you allow the person a place in your future or will you keep them a part of your past? If you choose to say goodbye, release them from a place of love, not anger. Let the words, "I do not wish to know you anymore" be carried by cleansing, gentle winds of springtime showers. Be grateful for the lesson. Be grateful for the healing.

Be grateful for your peace. Now, pick up your garden tools and celebrate. It's time to plant more dreams.

View forgiveness as a life lesson and an opportunity for you to gain wisdom and grow. Dig deep within and allow yourself to fully experience the hurt attached to the betrayal. Then grant yourself permission to move past the hurt, to release the person who caused it, and to experience the lightness of letting go. Focus on your growth, your peace, and your beautiful dreams.

Climbing Cliffs

"What I must do, is all that concerns me, not what people think."
~ Ralph Waldo Emerson

Cliff-Dwarf Primrose, also known as Smooth-leaf Douglasia, is a low-growing, stunning widflower that grows in mounds or clusters on mountain cliff faces. Their blooms are deep pink in color. If you climb high enough into mountainous terrain – places few have travelled – you will be rewarded with masses of astonishingly mesmerizing magenta-pink cliff primrose.

The climb toward blooms is symbolic of the climb you will take in search of your most valuable assets. Danger will surround you as you risk much to reach new heights and claim your prize. For just as wildflowers are temporary inhabitants of this world, so too is your life temporary. When you were young, you were the most "yourself," the most in-tune with your essence, embodying the gifts you were meant to share with the world. Perhaps you saw the world through a lens of innocence and simplicity, knowing that everyone you loved was alive and well inside your heart. As you aged, you evolved and growing in some ways, but withering and conforming in others. You may have battled against the dulling of your shine, but in order to survive, you may have taken on people-pleasing skills, caretaking jobs, and enabling performances. It's not your fault that you gave away pieces of your identity; you wanted love. You wanted acceptance. You wanted to belong. You learned to ignore the deep desires and the endless cravings of your own soul in order to accommodate the wishes of others.

Before your identity was solidified, you took on work that belonged to others. Time marched on and suddenly the innocence of your youth was shattered by watching those you loved suffer and struggle.

You experienced heartache. You lost cherished hearts to heaven. And you ached for a time when you saw everyone as decent, truthful, and honorable. Life unfolded in all of the unplanned ways that lives often do. You survived. You grew stronger – but also hardened. And you were shocked when you no longer recognized your reflection in the mirror, layered with filters that dulled your brilliance.

Still – you climbed cliffs. But the steepness that used to take your breath away began to frighten you.

Descending was even scarier. You stopped trusting yourself. You could no longer decide which rock to grab hold of or where to place your feet. The heart of your youth, that once held enormous wonders, was now steeped in layers of protection against those who would cause harm. And you knew with great certainty that the time had come to heal your heart, to shed heavy things, to connect to your truth, and to rediscover and claim the precious gifts that you thought you'd lost.

Begin your gift searching expedition. Stop betraying yourself. Shed the things that keep you tied to low places and ascend, without fear to the glorious cliffs you were meant to climb. The pretty, pink primrose is waiting for you.

Protect

Digging

"*Many times I say learn the art of love, but what I really mean is: learn the art of removing all that hinders love. It is a negative process. It is like digging a well; you go on removing many layers of earth, stones, rocks and then suddenly there is water. The water was always there; it was an undercurrent. Now you have removed all the barriers, the water is available. So is the love; love is the undercurrent of your being.*
It is already flowing, but there are many rocks, many layers of earth to be removed."

~ *Osho*

In life, there comes a time, when you will need to go digging. You will dig for things in your past that shaped, changed, or hurt you. You will dig for things in your present that no longer serve you, that rob your energy or take pieces of your soul. You will need to immerse yourself into digging for your beliefs and your spiritual self. You will dig to locate your place in this world and the beings you choose to accompany you on your journey.

Digging into your past is crucial because that is where things happened to you and changed you. You will need to understand how what happened to you in your past has affected you in your present. You will need to uproot those things in order to live your life unencumbered and move forward. There will be things that you have allowed to grow in your meadow. Perhaps you believed, at one time, that these things sustained you, assisted you, and made you better. But you now know that they only hindered and hurt you and so, they must go. These things present themselves in the form of people you've allowed close, circumstances you've endured, and habits you've adapted. It takes energy to recognize what needs to be dug up. And it takes commitment to do the work required to move ahead with the digging and to triumph over the uprooting.

Sometimes you need to target weeds or vines or bushes as you try desperately to dig up their roots and rid your life of their poison. Pay attention to when you're simply in search of a scapegoat, an easy target for blame. Many times, there is something much greater and deeper at work that you cannot allow yourself to acknowledge, and blaming another can seem easier than looking inside and accepting the fact that *you* need to change. Taking responsibility for things going amuck in your life and getting right with yourself may be beyond hard, but it is also beyond paramount. It is an essential part of living.

Just as important as finding out what to dig up and remove from your life is identifying which garden tool will perform such a task. Sometimes the soil is moist and the roots can be easily removed with whatever shovel or tool is at hand. Sometimes the ground is hard and impenetrable and the roots are deep and nasty and hard as steel beneath the earth. The sturdy, trusty shovel that worked magically in the past now breaks mercilessly into two, and you may find yourself winded, weary, and overwhelmed with the root removal. You feel the strength draining from you, as your knees buckle, your legs surrender and you fall helplessly to the ground.

And while you sit there, with your bottom melting into the earth and your spirit steeped in desperation, you get quiet. Pin. Drop. Quiet. It's from this place of leveling and groundedness that you begin to realize that you do not know how to dig up and remove things from your life in a proper fashion. You do not always have the strength. You do not always have the courage. And you do not always know what to remove and what to keep. And, damn it... your shovel is way too flimsy for the job at hand! From this low place, this grounded place, this place of surrender, you let go and ask God to help you find another way to live. He becomes your strength, your confidante, your advisor, your helper, your salvation... and your shovel.

In life, there are givers and takers, sunshine seekers and sunshine blockers, heart hurters and heart healers, back protectors and back stabbers, soul carriers and soul stompers, spirit purifiers and spirit poisoners. Stay close to the real. Steer clear of the fake. And remember always: when you know who you are, you will recognize who others are. And you will know, finally, what to dig up... and what to keep.

Intruders

"Let them go – the truthful liars and the false fair friends and the
boths and neithers – you must let them go
they were born to go."
~ e. e. cummings

The wildflower meadow is a shelter, a habitat, a sanctuary for
bees, butterflies, hummingbirds and all of nature to flourish.
There are weeds that although beautiful, are also noxious. They
can overpower the other blooms and interrupt cycles of nourishment and their survival. If you are planting your own garden
using a wildflower mix, beware of those that contain Queen
Anne's Lace, Toadflax, Bachelor's Buttons, Common Yarrow or
any other flowers that are ornamental yet aggressive. They will
undoubtedly overpower the other inhabitants.

Just as uninvited guests can intrude upon your meadow, so will uninvited guests appear in your life. These individuals enter the unguarded doorways of your days. They overtake. They overpower. They overwhelm. They attempt to gain control of your time, energy, and existence. Your life is precious. Your time and energy limited. Your goals and dreams need your attention, energy, and dedication in order to take root, grow, and flourish. If your vitality is spent ridding your life of intruders, you will have less time to populate the world with your essence and to help those who truly need you.

Intruders gain entry into your life when you experience moments of weakness and weariness. They dazzle. They hypnotize. They promise to inject beauty and brilliance into your world. Instead, they devastate and disappoint. They inject ugliness and darkness into what's inherently beautiful.

Protect yourself. Be vigilant in guarding the cracks in your life – the ones that formed when life overwhelmed you, when you failed to tend to your own needs, when things went missing. Make certain that tiny cracks do not become large chasms that make it possible for the wrong people and things to gain entry into your life.

Focus on your life and what it is trying to teach you. Focus on what may be missing from your life that allowed this intruder to gain access. Then... pick up your garden tools, put on your garden gloves and begin the removal work. Dig up the roots. Turn the soil. Pull the poison, the unwanted weedy people from your life.

Protect your wildflower life. Protect the sanctuary of your heart. Don't allow weeds to grow in your sacred spaces.

Traps

"I dig pits to trap others and fall in. I should be suspicious of what I want."

~ Rumi

The pitcher plant catches its prey by luring it with the scent of sweet smelling nectar. Insects are drawn to the promise of feasting on the nectar of the gods, only to be trapped on sticky hair follicles of the plant. The plant traps further by closing its' umbrella like lid. As the insect struggles to free itself, it expends great energy and exhaustion, which leads to its surrender and ultimate defeat.

As you journey on, living this human experience called life, you will encounter times when you feel as though you are missing something. Even though the truth is that you already have all that you need for your survival at your disposal, you will feel doubt. You will, at times, feel as though pieces of you are missing and lay scattered, far and wide. You will go on "missing pieces" expeditions, where you search endlessly for anything that can quell the hunger and the ache and provide you with the feeling of wholeness you crave. You may believe that reaching outside of yourself and pulling external things toward you will silence the longing that screams out from deep, hollowed-out heart places. You may feel a desperate need to silence the screaming, especially as it gets louder and louder with the passage of time.

Know that it is healthy to wander off your intended path, from time to time...to chase butterflies, to explore, to search for new experiences that provide well needed lessons to the business of living. But when you experience a powerful, internal ache that you cannot silence, you are most certainly receiving a warning of disconnection. If you cannot sit quietly with your own thoughts, without feeling an overwhelming urge to flee, you are in jeopardy of filling your life with things not meant for you.

When you are completely and utterly in sync with yourself and your creator, you have a feeling of internal peace and completeness. When you have done the work needed to truly forgive yourself, love yourself, and become your own best friend, you will feel connected and whole with no need to gravitate toward places of peril. Nothing will be missing.

Beware of things that distract you, captivate you, and lure you off of your chosen path. Many times, tempting things can damage the ability to think clearly. What appear to be twinkling stars burning brightly in the distance, filling your eyes with the hope and promise of wishes come true, may just be the searing, fiery flames of your demise. Stay the course. Don't stray. The urge to follow what lures you can also occur in the daytime, when you catch the faint scent of honeysuckle in the distance calling you to change direction. It can occur in the nighttime, when the harvest moon illuminates an object and causes curiosity and desire to well up inside you.

Veer off your path of belonging, if you must, from time to time. But do not sacrifice safe and sound for daring and dangerous. The choice to flourish or perish is yours alone. Do not allow yourself to be left defenseless – lulled by dishonorable intentions, captivated by charming masks, and imprisoned by tempting wiles. Make certain that you take inventory of what is inside you that may be yet unhealed. Sift through your own internal darkness. Look for places where you were left bludgeoned and bleeding, desperate and disappointed, forsaken and forgotten. Hurt can grow roots and overtake beauty, and so too can pain.

You can live a wildflower life from a place of goodness. The glitz and glory you seek, you already own. If you must risk, risk everything by shedding the armor you wear daily. Be courageous. Walk confidently with determination and purpose, knowing that you are planted exactly where you are meant to be in your meadow. Once you have made peace with yourself and are no longer accepting petal pieces of love in lieu of whole flowers and bouquets, be honest about your effect on others, the way you may have planted them in your life, what you wanted from them, and the way you tended to them or left them parched and begging for attention.

Make sure you impart your precious gifts to those nearest and dearest to you. Do not treat them as weeds to be pulled viciously from the earth, sprayed with poison, and discarded into the recycle bin of your life. Do not stand on mountaintops pointing fingers at everyone but yourself in a liar's paradise. Instead, take responsibility for your life. Look for your hurt. Dig deep until you find where it is buried. Use great strength to pull it from within, making sure to include the taproots. Respect and honor others and leave every being that enters your life fuller and finer than before you met them. Do great things from the place where you've been planted and know, in your heart... that this is where you belong. Blessed be.

Drink in the sweetness of your life. Don't get caught up in traps by searching for something sweeter. Dig deep into the painful parts of your life and do the work required to heal, so that you do not hurt or trap others because of unresolved pain that you carry. Respect and honor yourself and everyone around you. You have earned your place of belonging in the wildflower meadow.

Imposters

"If you can't smell the fragrance don't come into the garden of love, If you're unwilling to undress don't enter into the stream of truth. Stay where you are.
Don't come our way."
~ Rumi

Buttercups are often mistaken for yellow wild roses. Flowers often masquerade as other flowers and make identification difficult.

The life gifted to you requires that you do the work necessary to find your authentic self, your sacred self, your wild self. Buried deep within exists your truest truth – your most blessed blessedness waiting to be found and claimed. Each day you either journey closer to or further from your sacred self. Allow that which calls upon the retrieval of holiness to aid you in choosing those paths that lead you closer to your calling.

Things are standing in your way of this work. Fear denial, negativity, hopelessness, pain, disappointment, distraction, people-pleasing, and imposters will clog up the pathways to your sacred, wild soul. However, when you bring strength and commitment to your search, – the very things that derail you may also be used to ignite a fire that illuminates your course.

When an imposter enters your sphere and pretends to be in possession of an enormous heart, masquerading as a selfless spirit and a deep well of empathic energy, nothing real exists between you. There is no real friendship when there is deception. The mposter is, however, delivering wisdom in the form of a life lesson.

This encounter with the disingenuous will shake you to your core and hurt like hell, but you will survive. You will move past the hurt. You will come out on the other side of this counterfeit encounter, armed with tools to carry on with your sacred search of self.

Be honest with yourself about the qualities you revere. Make certain that these qualities truly exist in others and that you aren't simply wishing them present. Be honest with yourself about the light and dark that exists within you. You are human. Light and dark exists together. The choice is yours to lead with your light by living an authentic existence that enables you to pour goodness into the world.

Claim your gifts. Claim your truth. Claim your wild and sacred self. Stop shrinking your power. Stop dimming your light. Stop getting derailed by false things and fake prophets. Be yourself on purpose, without apology.

Step out of the darkness and into the lightness of your being and the essence of your truth. Tighten the boundaries around your wildflower heart and loosen the restraints that allow you to live authentically. Find the key that unlocks the doorway to your destiny. Live sacred. Live true. Live wild.

Dream Mowers

"Trust in dreams,
for in them is the hidden gate to eternity."
~ Khalil Gibran

Lady Bird Johnson, the wife of Lyndon B. Johnson, and the First Lady of the 36th President of the United States, focused much of her energy on the beautification of our nation, specifically on the highways, parks and places where masses of people pass. The mowing of wildflowers, along roadsides was discouraged and their growth encouraged.

When you have been gifted with a dreamer's soul, you view life through a lens of goodness, grace, and beauty. Dreamers possess a deep well of emotional generosity, paired with an ability to see beauty in everyone and everything. While this is certainly a blessing and something to be celebrated, it may also distort your ability to recognize those who enter your life with less than the purest of intentions. When you are wired to see goodness, when you are steeped in grace, it's easy to turn a blind eye to the ugliness that may exist in another.

In life, there will be those who think nothing of destroying beauty in their path. These people are "dream mowers" who stunt your growth, steal your idealism, and leave your life in disarray. Beware of shiny things in the distance that mesmerize and lull you into a trance, causing your defenses to drop, your mind to swim, and your body to sway. Meeting a dream mower can begin as a thrilling adventure that brings elation to your doorstep. You will experience a "Eureka, I struck gold" feeling, but emotions that flood and overwhelm also serve to dismantle your warning bells. Jolts of euphoria will move through you, catapulting you into a level of happiness so intense that you will orbit the sun, drenched in a trail of glitter and contentment, free from the worry of everyday life and on indefinite leave from the prison of mundane living. But those shiny, captivating qualities may well be shiny, sharp blades capable of mowing you down with great precision, leaving you incapacitated and permanently scarred.

You are special. You are blessed. You are heavily steeped in the business of helping. Know that there are those far from special, far from blessed, that are heavily steeped in the business of hurting. When they are near, you expend much energy questioning whether their actions are pure. You find yourself, slowly being lulled into their games and manipulation. You are here for a short time, meant to dream a million dreams, carry out a million different purposes and perform a million acts of kindness. The shiny things you see in the distance may not be wondrous things that will complete you and fill up the empty spaces you hold inside. They may in fact be sharp, steel blades intent on mowing down your most astonishing qualities.

Reserve your life energy. Store it for your own fortification, survival, and growth. Use your head, your heart, and your gut to weed out the "mowers of dreams", and do the work needed to shine brightly on the inside, so you no longer need to reach for shiny things…on the outside.

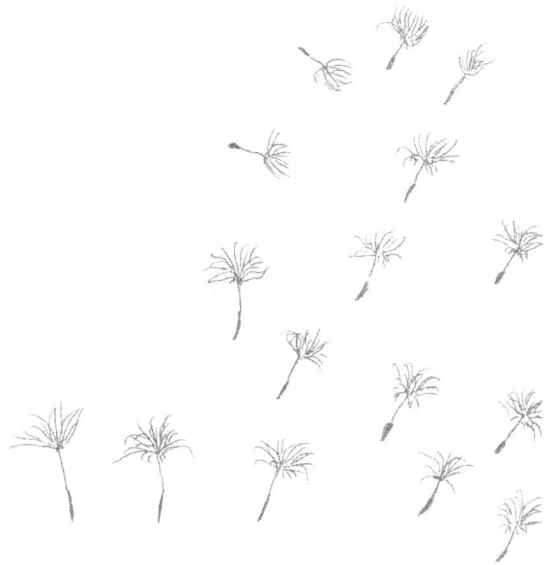

Meadow Mix

"The fragrance , my friends that floats to you this moment, streams from the tent of the Secrets of God."

~ Rumi

Wildflower meadows consist of flowers that grow without cultivation and are capable of surviving on their own without any intervention. A wildflower meadow holds space for every flower, every weed, and every growing condition and requirement needed.

Recognize those you are meant to grow next to in this world. Gather them toward you, as you would gather a bouquet of your favorite blossoms from the wildflower meadow. Arrange them into your days and allow their blooming bursts of light to deliver your lessons to you, to fill in your missing spaces with simple beauty, and to soothe the ache of being human. You will undoubtedly reach for and pull close, those you believe are your kindred souls. You will see them as friends you surely knew in another time and another place, for they seem familiar and wonderful and endearing. And they cause you to feel familiar and wonderful and endearing too. And so, you will draw them near, arrange them into your living, your breathing, your being. You will share your stories with them – the ones that live so deep inside you that they can only be accessed through the map of your soul. And you will trust them completely, love them totally, and usher them closely into the center of your heart.

You will be right in pulling them close and in remembering them as perfect soul companions. You will be right most of the time. But you will also be wrong, some of the time. And when this happens and when you discover the truth about their deception and their fake persona, you will be transported to a painful place where disappointment and disillusionment take seed and threaten to grow like a weed, overpowering all that you formerly knew to be good and true. You will question life. You will question love. You will question yourself. And the roots of distrust and hurt will take hold and be planted within you. You have some pain to go through. You have some learning to do. You have some weeding to do. You have some growing to do.

Keep your wildflower meadow, which represents the reality you have cultivated for yourself, clear of those who manipulate and make a mockery of life. Keep your meadow a haven for happiness and a place where love triumphs above the human tendency toward conflict, greed, resentment, and hatred.

Keep it a place where each step you take on the road that you travel leads you closer to a heart capable of feeling infinite amounts of love, a spirit filled with limitless joy, and a soul enlivened with God's perfect grace. Keep your meadow a place where your cherished relationships do not fade like the fragrance of flowers when the weather grows colder, but rather remain intact and vivid, emblazoned on your heart forever.

Keep your wildflower meadow a place that holds holy space for the sacredness of childlike innocence, when it was still possible and plausible to believe in the best of others. Keep it a place where you continue to learn and grow and strive to become your best self, but still leave room for falling short and being human. Keep it a place where you perform good deeds out of love and not for praise or elevated status. Keep it a place where you travel on paths intended for you, where you are greeted by your blessings as well as your hardships and that you have the insight to see both as instrumental to your growth and grace. Keep it a place where you are guided by a higher power to do the right thing followed by the next right thing and the next right thing, until a string of right things trails behind you as you move forward into your future.

Cultivate your life by choosing to weed out the unnecessary and the insincere that inhabit your world, take up space and pull you away from your destiny. Make room for more of what is meant for you, so you can live your life with meaning and passion and purpose.

Carrying Seeds

"Still here I carry my old delicious burdens, I carry them, men and women, I carry them with me wherever I go."
~ Walt Whitman

Bedstraws can be found growing in open fields. They consist of tiny flowers with four petals that fan out into layers of lace as they wind around low-creeping leaves and stems. Mixed in between the blossoms are oval-shaped seed pods covered in little hook-shaped fibers. The pods cling onto everything they touch and in this way, they catch a ride and are planted into many parts of the world.

Bedstraws are a reminder that on every path you travel, you'll meet souls you were meant to meet, witness beauty you were meant to absorb, and learn lessons you were meant to learn – provided you get close enough. You carry with you flower seeds of everyone you've ever encountered and shared precious time with. Your lungs expand with the same air that once circulated inside their lungs. You contain bits of every being you've connected with while walking this earth, their truths and cozy-campfire stories, tinged with smokiness. Your tongue tasted sweetness as they shared their triumphs; it tasted bitterness, as they poured out their sadness onto the caverns of your open heart. You carry the words of wisdom they imparted to you, so lovingly that they can still be heard in your mind when you need them most.

Continue to carry the things that help you on your journey. Sort through those things you carry inside that stuck to you like the brambles and bedstraws from wildflowers you hiked past. Sift through the rubble of what belongs to you, the things you absorbed that will help you with your future journey. Absorb the courage that makes you stronger, the lightness that eases burdens, the goodness that makes you holier.

Conversely, shed the things that don't align with your soul: bitter distrust, poisonous negativity, and crippling fear. Beware of those who compete with you and feign happiness for your successes. You will know them from the uneasy, anxious, and depleted feeling that swirls inside when they are near. Weed out the strangling vines that weigh you down, imprison you, and keep you from living wild and free. Think of toxic traits as weeds that threaten to overpower your glorious wildflower meadow. Don't allow hurt and negativity to take root and grow inside you. It's easier to pull weeds when the ground is still wet with salty tears from hurt hurled your way than from cracked, calloused ground. Dig deep, uproot poison, and discard that which you were never meant to carry – and become more capable and complete.

Carry only what makes you a more exceptional human. Allow those traits to take root within you, to blossom and flourish, so that they will grab hold of others when they pass and help them carry on. Toss the things you were never meant to carry. Lighten your load.

Share

Hidden Treasures

---

*"One's own self is well hidden from one's own self; of all mines
of treasure, one's own is the last to be dug up."*
~ Fredrich Nietzsche

The Nodding Wake-Robin is sometimes referred to as the Nodding Trillium, It is a low-growing, perennial plant that can be found thriving in the moistness of wooded, swampy forests. It has a single pure, white flower that blooms beneath three leaves and appears to nod, while hidden from sight. Native American Indians used to crush the leaves of this plant and make an herbal remedy for skin irritations and bug bites. This plant is extremely rare and may be considered endangered in many states.

This wildflower reminds you that you are rare and extraordinary. You came to this earth carrying a treasure trove of gifts. You may have always been aware of these unique gifts, or they may have been hidden, just as the leaves of the Nodding Wake-Robin hide its blossoms. You may have to do some digging work to unearth your precious, hidden things. Many times, the distractions of life force you to forfeit blocks of time chasing things within sight that are deemed necessary. You may feel as though you should be achieving more, doing more, seeing more. You place enormous pressure upon yourself adhering to what society considers valuable and beautiful; usually these are in plain sight.

The superficial parts of living absorb chunks of your waking hours, just as images of perfection bombard your senses. You are told to pour your miraculous, curvy body into impossibly, narrow fitted garments. You are given the message that the deep lines imprinted on your lovely face, lines reflecting moments lived of ecstasy and anguish, should be erased, if you wish to be viewed as valuable in society. As a result, you are left feeling that you are somehow less than, as you attempt to live up to an unrealistic, unattainable, and unhealthy expectation of beauty. If you buy into external opinions of beauty instead of creating and believing in your own, you will not be living your truth. You will never find your own beauty and you will never discover your own internal treasures.

The truth is that you are beautiful. You are worthy. You fit in. You don't have to change. You don't have to become something that you are not. You don't have to spend your life moments emulating others. You are here to find your hidden treasures, to unearth your loveliness, to uncover your potential. and to share your rare gifts with the world. You are exactly where you need to be. You are learning what you need to learn. Your circumstances, your appearance, your personality, all serve as vehicles to learn, to grow and to expand your horizons.

The external things are limited and finite. The internal things make you real and limitless and infinite. The things you cannot see are the things that make you rich beyond wealth or material possessions. You are unique and cherished and loved by many. Recognize the rare gifts that you shelter and hide away beneath your leaves – the pure, white flower gifts that are blooming inside you – hidden from sight. Brush away the distractions, the ways you shield your true identity, the leaves that loom above you and keep you nodding, conforming and hidden from sight. Strip yourself of everything, until you are naked, raw, real... you. And know that *you are wondrous.*

Uncover the truth of who you are. Separate yourself from all the man-made distractions. Reject cloaking yourself in anything that doesn't feel authentic to you. Nod to the hidden and holy things that are meant to be discovered, set free, and shared.

Senses

"We are all in the gutter, but some of us are looking at the stars."

~ Oscar Wilde

Sweet Alyssum is a low-growing plant that belongs to the mustard family. It bears tiny, clustered flowers in lavender, pink, and white. It possesses a strong, sweet, fragrance that attracts ladybugs. The meaning of this blossom is grace, wonder, and worth beyond beauty.

Wildflowers awaken your senses to a world of wonder. They add layers of beauty, instill hope into your heart and stir up a passion for all that is real and alive. Use your God-given senses to recognize yourself in the wildflower meadow – the earth you inhabit. See the vivid hues of colors merge and meld, just as the rays of sunshine cast shadows on the petals and the wind makes them perform their freedom dance, as though their roots do not tether them to the earth at all. Watch as the varying conditions supplied by Mother Nature affect them. Storms make them look wonderful or weary. Temperatures cause a heavenly aroma to rise, stir your memory, and remind you of a place that exists in a faraway paradise. A place that used to be and will be again...your true home. A place that holds the loved ones you ache to hold again. Watch as the haunting raindrops cause delicate plants to glisten, drenching their parched petals. Listen to their joy, as grace rises up and bursts from them in shouts of mad glory.

You were placed here, on this soil, on this planet, on this plane to be a "lover of happily ever after." Claim your place here and wrap your arms around all of the "hallelujah moments" you experience. Remember to be a kind and giving human. Continue to grow, evolve, and cling tightly to the good instilled within at your time of creation. Don't fall prey to the comparison game – holding your accomplishments, appearance and attributes up against others. Don't be misled into believing that others are above the human condition. Every being has moments of glory, contentment, and sheer joy, as well as moments of lowliness, misery, and melancholy.

Make an effort to help every soul you encounter because fate is not happenstance – and what seems like chance is never coincidence. The gifts you and you alone contain can help and heal others. Pour your heart into the hearts of others, for the love you share is golden and not a silly, fairy tale.

Know yourself. Share yourself. Give of yourself. For it is in giving that broken things are made whole and it is in sharing that unlovely things are made lovely. You are worthy of inhabiting this field of flowers, this earth – where you walk and run and dance and sometimes trudge. Know that your generous, loving heart certainly makes you a thing of wondrous beauty.

Use your senses to experience the wonder that lay waiting for you to discover. Help others by igniting a passion within them, so they can experience the joys of their life. Don't just root for yourself on your journey. Root for everyone and wrap your heart around every precious moment of your life.

Butterfly Dreams

"All people dream, but not equally. Those who dream by night in the dusty recesses of their mind, wake in the morning to find that it was vanity. But the dreamers of the day are dangerous people, for they dream their dreams with open eyes, and make them come true."

~ D. H. Lawrence

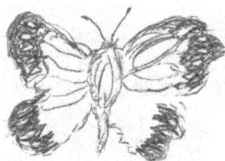

Butterflies have eyes that consist of six-thousand lenses. They have ears that are capable of hearing. Their tongues are shaped in a long, tube-like shape, so they can soak up their food from nectar on flowers that may be difficult to reach. Their wings, although colorful to behold, are actually clear, with the colors and patterns coming from reflections of tiny scales they are covered in. They sometimes travel in a group – called a flutter.

Butterflies are profound wonders of nature, with much to

teach us. To dream of butterflies is to receive a calling to share your ideas and your truths with the world. Let these magical creatures be a reminder of what you need to do in this life. Butterflies have an incredibly short life span. When you witness this flying flower of nature with gossamer wings fluttering near, let it serve as a reminder to share your beauty with others. Remind yourself to flutter with grace near those in need of your understanding, your inspiration, your comfort and your love.

Contribute prolifically like the butterfly. Pollinate people with your warmth and fly higher than you believe possible, past buildings that scrape the sky and mountains that poke at pearly heavenly gates. Remind yourself to persevere when fear threatens to overtake you and causes great trembling in your fragile, butterfly body. Find your bliss in the meadow of life and be still long enough to drink in its sustaining, sweet nectar. Although you cannot witness your own beauty, others can; they'll rejoice in your elegance and gasp with delight at the outward markings of your body that reflect and resemble the inner markings of your soul.

Traveling unencumbered allows you to move more easily through the stages of growth and time. Remind yourself that the way you begin your journey will be altered in unexpected ways by a million, unplanned happenings. The plans you have made for yourself will most certainly be derailed by the plans that God has in store for you. Surrender to the hallowed and holy changes you undergo or you will surely lose yourself in the great struggle against them.

Remind yourself to absorb the warm rays of sunlight before the darkness creeps in. Change your flight pattern from time to time and know you are capable of adjusting to new ways of moving through the world. Scan your horizon for danger, but know that you are a true survivor capable of flying with missing pieces of your wings. Remind yourself that pain of loss is needed to grow, the agony of boredom is needed to find your center, and the carrying of burdens is needed to gather strength.

Remind yourself that your life is a journey toward your transformation and the emergence of your glorious gifts. Dream of butterflies. Fear nothing. Feel everything… and fly.

Daisy Days

"Not worlds on worlds, in phalanx deep, need we to prove a God
is here; The daisy, fresh from nature's sleep, tells of
His hand in lines as clear."
~ John Mason Good

Daisies are considered a vascular plant. They are capable of distributing nutrients and water all throughout the entire plant. The white petals constitute one flower and the yellow, pollen center counts for another.

Perhaps there is no greater symbol for happiness, peacefulness, and childlike exuberance than the beloved daisy. It's quite impossible to let sadness live inside you when you encounter a field of pure white petals with sunshine yellow centers, perched on stems that billow in the warm breeze.

Live your life according to the way of the daisy. Allow the magic of your childhood to bubble up inside you and over-shadow the struggles of adulthood. Be lighter and more carefree. Approach all your days as moments where simplicity, gratitude, and miracles collide to create your one unique and precious life.

Live your life according to the way of the daisy. Remain posi-tive by refusing to absorb cruelness. When someone spews venom in your direction, don't let it in. It is merely their self-loathing and internal darkness looking for a place to take root. Choose to be a "walking on air," satisfied person, not a "hands and knees" disgruntled one.

Be generous with your time, your money, your support, and your kind words – and know that those who are selfish with these things will be selfish with their heart as well. Givers ex-ude love. Takers steal it. Keep things simple by mentally strip-ping away your self image, as well as how you believe others perceive you. Strip away your material possessions, your home, your vehicle, your jewelry, your bank account. Remove your masks and reveal the nakedness of your God-given, luminous face. Release the power that you have come to believe you own. Surrender to the purity of your soul and spirit.

With loving, accepting eyes, look at your reflection. Do you like what you see? Are you enough, without all the clutter and material things you have accumulated in layers, hiding your true self? You are more than enough. You are heaven sent. You were placed on this earth for a million reasons. You have power within you to make a difference in this world, to elevate it to a higher and holier level. The world needs your wild-flower ways. Live out all your daisy days by filling others with goodness, kindness, and inspiration. And above all, be true to yourself and love from the depths of your grateful and fearless heart.

Pattern your life after the daisy, with simplicity, purity, and lightness of being.

Evening Primrose

"*The only gift is a portion of thyself.*"
~ Ralph Waldo Emerson

The lemon-colored, lemon-scented petals of the Evening Primrose prefer to bloom at sunset, when night-flying moths are drawn to them. The flower is believed to store sunlight inside its petals, causing a luminosity to be given off in the darkness, attracting pollinators to their sweet, fragrant gifts.

Your gifts can also be found in the quiet stillness of the dark, when the whispers of daylight are amplified in your ears. If you are uncertain about what your gifts are, look to the places in life where your passion swells. Look to the voices of those you hold close. They will offer compliments surrounding those gifts. You may be too close to discern what your gifts are. You may be too doubtful about your accomplishments and lack the confidence to grab hold of your talents and cultivate them. Remember you can be both humble and confident.

Rest assured you are a spiritual creature filled with heavenly treasures, bestowed upon you by your Maker, with the plan for you to ignite passion with your paintings, soothe souls with your music, and populate the garden of earth with your words of inspiration. Follow whatever tugs at your heart, whatever pulls you closer to divinity, whatever breathes life into the mundane.

Recognize the moments in time that reduce you to pure passion. What was the vehicle that stirred your senses, brought you to your knees, caused you to forget your sadness, and made you fall in love with your sweet, fragrant, primrose life?

Get comfortable with the gifts inside you. Don't worry about appearing boastful for possessing them. Don't try to dull their brilliance. Be bold about finding them, owning them, and sharing them freely. Give those gifts to others, and you'll attract back to you what you need within yourself. The more you work on cultivating your gifts, the more sunlght they give off, and the more others will be drawn to you. Let your gifts heal the hurting, restore the hopeless, and ignite a burning passion in others to find their gifts. Share your talents and fall, hopelessly, desperately and madly in love with being alive.

Find your gifts in the stillness of the dark. But share your gifts in the whirlwind of the light. Use them to restore healing and hope to the world and cause everyone in your wake to love their life – just a little more.

Hummingbird Wisdom

"Knowing yourself is the beginning of all wisdom."
~ Aristotle

Hummingbirds appear in the wildflower meadow, like enchanted guardian spirits – with their brightly colored, tiny fairytale wings – flapping in the wind twelve to ninety times per second. Their miniscule heart beats at a rate of 1,260 beats per minute. They fly faster than any bird in the heavenly sky. Their high metabolism demands enormous amounts of nutrition to support the rapid fire intensity of their flying and flitting. They are capable of flying backwards as well as forwards. They are attracted by the color of flowers – unlike insects, which are attracted by the fragrance. Bright shades of pink, purple, yellow, orange and red blooms draw the hummingbird ever close.

These enchanted wildflower meadow dwellers have much to teach us with regard to living a life worthy of the sacred heart that beats within. When you spot one of these magical creatures, you are drenched in awe at their beauty and the way they move through the air. Hummingbirds are attracted to flowers that provide sweet nectar for their survival. When they hover near their source of nourishment, they teach us to stay close to what fortifies the gifts of spirit. A life steeped in miracles requires constant feeding to keep your goals and dreams alive.

Hummingbirds are magically drawn toward bright blooms. A powerful force constantly draws you toward bright places that provide perfect promises for your dreams to take flight. Be brave when you feel this pull. Allow yourself the freedom to fly with exuberance toward bursts of color that lead you closer to your divinity. Do not be afraid or resist, but rather drink in the sweet nectar of your life. Collect the sun-drenched pollen and deliver its magic to the world as only you can.

Hummingbirds are capable of flying both forward and back-ward, reminding you to be flexible while moving through life. Moving forward is crucial to carrying on and meeting your glorious destiny. Moving backwards is needed to assess your progress and gain access to a broader picture of life's patterns and choices – so you aren't simply losing energy hovering near dead-end things that don't allow you to claim your gifts and share your soul.

Celebrate the glorious mystery of your short stint in this world. Stay close to everything and everyone that provides nourishment for your survival, fuel for your talents and pathways to pollinate the world with your God-given brilliance.

Pint-Sized Perfection

"From a little spark may burst a flame."
~ Dante Alighieri

Deptford Pink, or Grass-Pink, is a tiny, wildflower that blooms in the late spring and stays until the late autumn month of October. It is a grass-like plant that holds a miniscule, pretty, pink flower. Although small in size, the flower is awe-inspiring to behold. The blossom has five delicate, yet intricately pointed petals – graced with tiny, white spotted dots, near the center.

The miniscule size of this wildflower demonstrates that the smallest things sometimes have the power to cause the biggest tug to our heart strings. When you see this diminuitive, pink-petal plant growing in clusters that hug low to the ground, you will certainly stop, gasp, and be overcome with wonder.

Let this tiny flower be a reminder to you, that small things done with big love have the capacity to take up enormous space inside the hearts of the desperate and weary. Sitting with someone in their sorrow, visiting them where they dwell in a grief-filled room, logging long hours, living out a prison sentence of pure pain with invisible iron bars, that keep them locked away, pining for the feeling of a lost heartbeat...all of this may well be the greatest gift you can give another. Sharing your affection, your essence, and your natural inclination to comfort may seem insignificant, but just like the pretty pink grass flower that leaves you drenched in awe, your small act of kindness coats others with a healing light that soothes their soul.

If you hold within you the gift of healing, you will be pulled by an invisibly strong and magnetic force toward those that have suffered crushing defeats. You will recognize their attempts to hang on, low to the ground, near rock-bottom painful places, trying desperately to carry on with the business of living and loving. Meet them where they are. Gather up your gifts of compassion and nurturing and healing and wrap them tightly within the petals of your heart. Allow them to dwell there, while you carry on with your day-to-day tasks. Tell them your stories, when they are unable to speak. Lend them your ear when their words begin to surface. Nurture them with your tenderness. Hug them with your heart. Provide them a safe place to rest until their pain slightly lessens, their limbs start to move again, and their eyes, once blurred with tears, begin to open until they are once again able to focus on the crushing beauty of their own pink-petal, awe-drenched, and wondrous life.

Pour your gift of nurturing onto the hurting hearts that you encounter. Heal them with your comfort. Release them from their prison of grief. Allow tiny wonders to blossom into enormous miracles.

Scattered Seeds

"All your thoughts, all the seeds scattered by you, perhaps for-
gotten by you, will grow up and take form. He who has received
them from you will hand them on to another. And how can you
tell what part of you may have in the future determination of
the destinies of humanity?"
~ Fyodor Dostoyevsky

Wildflower seed packets have replaced the traditional rice
throwing at weddings. Seed packets are formulated for differ-
ent growing regions. Many contain baby's breath, cornflowers,
cosmos, daisies, blackeyed susans, lupine and rose mallow.

Each flower seed is a promise of new life, a future vision of
untamed beauty that will grace the earth – not to mention a
much needed oasis for butterflies, bees, and all of nature to
visit and feed upon. Flowers are beacons of beauty that restore

the hope of wholeness to a desperately fractured world.

You also possess this healing power inside. When you release the unnecessary, the frivolous, and the cumbersome things that you lug around and that weigh you down, you create conditions for opportunities to help and heal. Lightening up allows you to propel forward, meet others where they are planted, and share precious seeds of wisdom with them.

When you help others for the sole purpose of being of service, with no personal gain as a goal, you are doing God's work. When you become a vessel of good intentions and scatter good deeds onto the waiting world, you are sowing a life rich with beauty. And what bursts through the earth is pure and decent: Help, for the sole purpose of helping. Resist the urge to inform the world of your deeds, for that in turn feeds your ego, as the world sees you as a good doer and offers praise, which ego absorbs and thrives upon. Keep the scattered seeds of your actions pure. Gather every vestige of energy and help raise humanity to a higher and holier place, without expectation of anything in return.

Be of service to all that you are able to help. Enlighten those that may have gone dark in faith. Sweeten those that have bitterness on their tongue from swallowing too many disappointments. You cannot save the crestfallen, suffering souls that you meet on your journey. But you can open your soul and let the holy things inside spill onto them. You can open your mouth and let warm words of encouragement tumble forth to offer comfort. You can open your heart and let the love that pours from it bathe aching hearts in rays of hope that bring promise to the end of their struggle.

Make room inside you for the carrying of precious things. Line your pockets with good deeds and good intentions Scatter seeds of goodwill. Sprinkle all the beauty that you carry within, just as you would sprinkle packets of flower seeds onto the hungry, waiting soil. Perform simple acts of kindness with great love. Know that the small things you do daily, the repeated giving of yourself - allow the seeds of your identity to scatter and set the stage for enormous wonders to take root in others. Don't miss an opportunity to share yourself, to help others, and to give to others. Through giving, you become more real, more selfless, and *more wild.*

Share yourself with others. Help others become happier, healthier and more whole. Help them find their wild. Spread your wildflower ways. The world is waiting… to be healed.

Signs

*"Dwell on the beauty of life. Watch the stars, and
see yourself running with them."*
~ Marcus Aurelius

*The Cardinal flower, sometimes referred to as Red-Betty,
is perhaps the most brilliantly colored and most showy of all the
wildflowers. It grows in shady, moist woods, shedding bright
red hues in the darkest corners of the forest. The fiery color is an
invitation for birds to gather and feast.*

The cardinal bird, after which these blooms are named, is
famous for being viewed as a sign from a heavenly world, one
that delivers messages of hope. When you see one of these
bright, red birds, have faith that someone you lost to heaven
is sending messages of love. The blossom and the bird are a
reminder that things of richness, brilliance, and beauty often
grow in dark places – where the sun's rays cannot reach.

When the difficulty of life threatens to extinguish your light and deliver you into the darkness, take comfort in knowing you are never alone. The air you inhale is the air that God exhales. The heart that beats inside your chest is a heart connected to dwellers of heaven that once walked the earth beside you. Each footstep you take is followed by the footsteps of those you have loved and lost. There is a constant flow of celestial signs being sent from the world in which you originated and flooding the space you inhabit.

Stay open to signs, for they provide you with strength to carry on, to overcome your struggles –reminders that God's grace is ever-present. Each challenge that you encounter and over-come makes you stronger, wiser, and more resilient. It is in the darkness that your gifts and talents are formed and cultivated. Be brave when facing your fears and when overcoming the obstacles and hardships placed in your path. Your courage will be rewarded with a deepening of your beauty, your talents, and your gifts; these, too, are ever-present, waiting to be found, cultivated, and shared. Believe in yourself and know that you are worthy of the gifts bestowed upon you. Allow those gifts to blossom and burst open from the deepest places inside you – so they may spread far and wide, reach the darkest, unconse-crated corners of the world, and bathe others in a healing, holy light.

You are unique to the universe. You are a rare, red cardinal flower blooming in a deep, dark, woody world. There will be times in life when you will feel defeated, deflated, and filled with sadness. You must never lose hope. The darkness of the woods provides you with opportunity to shed the trivial, worldly things that encumber you and weigh you down. Once emptied out, you can connect to the glow of your inner light. It burns brightly inside the chambers of your heart. It provides strength. It provides direction. It provides peace. It envelopes you in warmth until fear and sadness subside. Allow your internal gifts and your inner light to shine brightly – so they can lead you to your perfect path and shed light on everyone's darkness.

The world needs your gifts, your love… your holy light.

Bloodroot Sensitivity

"All can hear, but only the sensitive can understand."
~ Khalil Gibran

Bloodroot is an early, spring bloomer. The stem bursts through the ground in early May, followed by a single leaf that wraps around the stem and emerging bud almost as though it were giving a protective hug. When the bud is ready to burst forth, it is pushed upward by the stalk, but the single leaf remains in a surrounding stance, still guarding. Bloodroot possesses seven to twelve pure white, delicate petals. Many of these flowers have difficulty enduring heavy wind or rain and most do not survive past a day or two in full bloom. The bloodroot flower is considered a delicate, sensitive one. Bloodroot symbolizes healing, growth, love, protection, and sensitivity.

To be bestowed with sensitivity is a beautiful gift, one the world will undoubtedly judge as a weakness. You may falsely believe that ruthlessness is the key to your success, as if sensitivity is something to conquer.

The truth tells a different story. If you are a highly sensitive person, you hold within you a multitude of gifts that will shape your life and shed light on your purpose – provided you learn the art of channeling those gifts and the self-care that will help you sustain them.

Sensitivity should be celebrated, not cursed. Being a tender-hearted being in a soul-slamming world is, at times, an unbearable burden. But you are alive in ways that others are not. You have the capacity to see beauty where others see foul and possibility where others see despair. You feel everything. You love everyone. All of your senses and experiences are heightened and your life is ablaze with passion and gratitude. When you feel sorrow, it envelops you, causing crumbling in the walls of your heart until you fall to your knees in surrender. When you feel joy, it shoots through your body, fireworks causing wings to sprout from your shoulder blades, until you fly, close to heaven, where your essence lives. You are a creative soul, capable of healing, helping, and heaping enormous amounts of love into a love-starved world. You possess a deep well of empathy, which emboldens you to willingly carry the weary and broken-hearted.

The challenge? Believing in and cultivating your most precious gifts. This will nourish you, sustain you, and encourage growth. Stay close to all that is sacred and seek security from your higher power through the direct line of your heart. Protect yourself by surrounding yourself with those that love you, just as the leaf of the bloodroot plant surrounds and protects its bursting bud.

Be brave. Be giving. Be open. But shelter yourself from darkness, for you are light and porous and easily absorb dark and heavy things. Embrace your sensitive soul. Allow your creativity to flow freely through unblocked channels, so it can surface and be shared. Allow yourself rest when life overwhelms you. Allow yourself to grieve when pain envelops you. And allow yourself to celebrate when joy reaches the beautiful treasure trove of gifts you carry – so that the big love you find impossible to contain is able to burst forth and bathe the world in your beautiful light.

You are a giver. Give. You are a creator. Create. You are a healer. Heal. You are a lover. Love.

Remember

Forget-Me-Nots

"Silently, one by one, in the infinite meadows of heaven, blossom the lovely stars, the forget-me-nots of the Angels."
~ Henry Wadsworth Longfellow

Forget-Me-Nots are charming, tiny blue flowers with a yellow ring at the center that serves to attract bees for pollination. This endearing blossom is the official state flower of Alaska, as well as the popular lead in many stories.

Throughout the ages, tales about these legendary blossoms have circulated. A Christian legend claims that after Adam and Eve ate the apple but before they were banished from Paradise, this delicate, five-petal, star of a flower called out to them: "Forget me not." A popular superstition claims that if lovers wore strands of these tiny flowers around their necks, they'd never be forgotten by their beloved.

Unforgettable people enter doorways of your life in such profound ways that even if they exit, never to appear again, you carry the imprint of them deep in your heart. A vision of them is stored, like a cherished, framed photograph, in the crevices of your mind. Their essence lingers like the fragrance of your favorite flower and will follow you throughout the duration of your days.

As you live out the different chapters of your life, something familiar will trigger a memory of them that you believed had faded with the passage of time. Without warning, their smiling face will flash across the screen of your mind and a memory of a well-spent, summer day will surface. During your most difficult days, when nothing makes sense and you are washed in sadness and feeling defeated, their voice will echo inside you, like a devastatingly beautiful song you had long forgotten but never stopped loving. You will feel that they have returned to you as their spirit wraps around you, fills you with warmth, and restores you back to a hopeful state.

Forget-me-not flowers remind you that beautiful relationships are manifestations of love and love doesn't fade the way memory does. Love lives on in the hearts and souls of those who have experienced it. Deep connections are born of the spirit, blessed by God, nurtured by moments lived, and kept alive inside your heart. Quiet your mind. Stop your body from stirring.

Stay open to those that have showered your soul with affection, connected you to your inner source, and deposited massive amounts of love into your heart. When you need them most, remember them, picture them, feel them and listen for them, for they are near, whispering softly and sweetly... "Forget-me-not".

Forget-Me-Not people are like sweet flowers pressed into the pages and days of your life. Draw strength from the wisdom they imparted to you and the love they gave you. And never, ever allow yourself to forget.

Lavender

"Be clearly aware of the stars and infinity on high. Then life
seems enchanted after all. If you truly love nature,
you will find beauty everywhere."
~ Vincent van Gogh

Lavender is a popular, well-loved plant. A member of the mint family, the blooms are produced on long spikes that are adorned with flowers that range in color from pale lilac to deep purple, but can also be found in shades of pink, red, and white. Lavender loves full sun and hates too much water. The plant has no natural enemies, no animals that munch on its flowers, leaves or woody stems. The scent emitted from lavender deters most insects and can be sprayed on the skin as an insect repellant before a nature walk. Lavender oil can be dropped into bath water or mixed with water and sprayed onto pillow cases to invite sleep and sweet dreams.

In the world of flowers, lavender means devotion, luck, success, and happiness. Lavender reminds you to slow down your harried pace, to be fully present for each moment, and to savor its sweetness. Witnessing the sight of pale purple blanketing rolling hills brings a feeling of peace and enchantment. The heady fragrance of the blossoms can transport you to a place that provides respite from the frenzy of the world. In the quiet of the meadow, you can hear whispers of glorious things. You can feel a stirring deep inside your soul and commune with your true essence.

Life is chaotic and fast-paced. Being constantly bombarded with images, communication, and stimulation sometimes drowns out what really matters. Lavender is a reminder of the calm, the quiet, the peaceful space that exists between all the madness. Visiting that space makes it possible to commune with the creator of all things, to get in touch with the essence of your identity and to connect with the beautiful bounty of gifts you possess. Let lavender remind you to slow down and to create pockets of space in your days that deliver moments of sweet surrender and relaxation. Allow those emptied out spaces to be filled with heavenly and holy things – not of this world.

Lie in a field of lavender. Breathe in the sweet fragrance. Calm your mind. Soothe your soul. Find your center. And without all the clatter and clutter of this world, bask in your truth and allow yourself to remember... who you truly are

Moments

*Buttercups resemble tiny bursts of sunshine, clustered together.
The most common buttercup variety is called Ranunculus acris.
It grows tall in moist meadows, roadsides and on neighborhood
lawns. Its leaves are pointy shaped and resemble the large foot
of a bird. Although sweet to look at, buttercups are actually
quite bitter and can even cause blisters on hands when picking
them. The bitterness may have evolved as a defense mechanism
for survival against meadow-grazing animals.*

Buttercups evoke cherished moments of childlike surrender,
when a friend would hold the waxy, golden blossom under-
neath your chin to look for the reflection of yellow on your

skin, revealing your love of butter. Imagine collecting all the miraculous moments of your life, just as you would gather gorgeous blooms from a meadow. Envision your very existence as running wild and free in a field filled with rich, luscious-colored blossoms in different hues, shades, and intensity. Some carry a heady fragrance, while others smell like the promise of spring clinging to their little plant bodies. Be overwhelmed by the sheer intensity of their grandeur.

The meadow symbolizes your life and its myriad blooms represent your gifts. See your body as a vessel to fill up, a flower basket readied to be full with the experience of living. Take your basket body and run as fast as your adventure-seeking legs carry you. Feel the soft, velvety blanket under your bare, summer feet, feel the swell of sensation as your skin comes alive when the taller plants reach out and tickle you as the breeze lifts. Fill up with the potpourri of petals that your eyes feast upon: wild roses for love, violets for innocence, lavender for peace, Gay feather bursting with color and reminding you of the stardust you'll someday become.

Honor the simple moments of your life. Be open to them. Look for them. Count them among your blessings and be grateful. The simple moments that you fill yourself up with hold the key that unlocks the wonder and magic of living an exceptional life. Surrender to simplicity: wandering walks without a destination, the silent, sweet tug of your heartstrings when you see an old friend after many years apart. Inhale the aroma of freshly baked bread, the kind your mother used to make that tasted like home and made you feel loved. Honor the moments that allowed you to find your talents and made others feel loved because you shared them. Before your one precious life expires, your memory fades, like an old photograph that lost its color, causing you to forget the names and faces of your magical loves. Before your body breaks down, wastes away with bones that creak like floorboards from a home built long ago, gather all of your moments, your gifts, your love...everything that together makes up your life.

Before you, a meadow of wildflowers. Recognize the simple moments that are strung together to form the miraculous gift of your extraordinary, blessed and beautiful wildflower life.

Dandelion Wishes

*"He, who wishes to secure the good of others, has
already secured his own."*
~ Confucius

*The dandelion enters the scene in early spring but stays far
longer than any other flower. It is a member of the composite
family of flowers – made up of one to two hundred tiny tube-
like flowers, clustered together. Their deep green, tender leaves
are packed with nutrition and have graced many salad bowls.
The yellow blossoms are often plucked from their stems in early
spring and made into a delicious wine. Although beautiful, dandelions remain the most controversial in the weed-flower debate.*

Folklore surrounding this wildflower claims that English children of the 20 th century believed that the white, puffy seeds
that flew through the air were actually fairies that could make

their wishes come true, if at first caught and then set free.

The dandelion uses the wind to transmit seeds and because of this, possesses the most efficient way to guarantee propagation. They are the masters of seed spreading and can travel extremely long distances. Each dandelion seed is accompanied by a downy, puffy piece of soft angel wing as a travel companion. These move freely on the wind, serving as messengers of beauty and reminders of time spent immersed in childhood innocence and backyard and playground wishes. In full bloom, dandelions carpet open patches of grass with a sprinkling of bright yellow sunshine. When the wind blows, their golden heads seek you out, as their scalloped leaves open, like out-stretched arms searching for a hug.

When deciding whether to pull them from the ground or wish upon them, look to their color. The white of the dandelion clock – seed state - symbolizes intelligence, purity, and soul/spirit survival. Yellow symbolizes clarity of thought, communication, growth, joyfulness, and healing. Yellow is also a fire color, which brings warmth, brilliance, and clarity. The meaning of the two colors merge yearly over a sweet, decadent birthday cake, adorned with mini, blazing, multicolored wax wishing totem poles. And as your hopeful breath blows and reaches the flame of each waiting candle, your miracle wish reaches a sovereign being that reigns quietly over all the moments of your life. Before the smoke clears, a new plan is inspired and set into motion.

A wish is your soul's way of communicating things you are meant to do. Recall the wishes of your childhood, for they live inside you and transform into the dreams of your adulthood. Set them in motion, just as the dandelion seed blows through the air, like a mini parachute awaiting its landing. Allow your wishes to take flight, land in your heart and make your dreams come true.

May Apple

"The only gift is a portion of thyself."
~ Ralph Waldo Emerson

May Apple, also known as the umbrella plant, gets its name by blooming in the earliest month of spring. They grow deep in the woods and their shiny, green leaves look like a cluster of umbrellas, popping up on the forest floor. Though the leaves are quite conspicuous, round in shape with 57 lobes, the two-inch white flower, as well as the lemon-shaped fruit that it bears, is hidden deep beneath the leaves. The fruit that grows can take up to four years to ripen. Once it reaches its prime, it is pure perfection, delightful in taste and sweet in aroma.

The lengthy time process that the May Apple takes to bear its luscious, aromatic fruit reminds you that you may need to travel long on the road that leads to your gifts and talents. The journey, however, is more than worth it. If you have yet to discover the depth of your God-given gifts, then you are missing out on the richness that your life holds. Your gifts are unique to you alone. If you need help identifying the special things that live inside you, look to the activities that stir up ridiculous amounts of passion within, provide escape from the dullness and darkness of life, and bring you a feeling of euphoria.

Remember the days of your childhood and recall the activities that made your heart leap with joy until everything else faded away and you felt utterly alive and totally present. Special things live inside you. They wait patiently for you to search, past mountains and meadows, past trials and tribulations, past endless days and countless years. They are waiting, deep in the woods – deep in your soul, hidden from sight, sheltered under crisp, green umbrella plant leaves, hoping for the day when you claim them, tend to them, and share them with the world.

Once you claim your gifts, become comfortable with them. Get to know them. Peel the clustered layers back slowly and relish each glorious part. Be patient with their unfolding and with their cultivating. Wrap yourself in those layers and incorporate them into your daily practice, until they become like the ripened, sweet fruit of the May Apple. And with open hands and an open heart...serve them up to the magical loves of your life.

137

Surrender to the sacredness of gifts that are yours to claim. Don't stop searching for them. Don't give up hope that you have them. Their magic will invigorate you, ignite a fire within you, and place you on the path of joy.

Ghost Gifts

"You hide me in your cloak of nothingness. Reflect my ghost in your glass of being. I am nothing, yet appear: transparent dream where your eternity briefly trembles."

~ Rumi

The Indian Pipe or Ghost Plant can be found growing deep in forests. Shaped like the bowl of a pipe, it has no chlorophyll and cannot produce its own food. It relies on its parasitic relationship with trees and fungus for survival. The plant can be found growing near decaying tree stumps and mushrooms. It has no fragrance to attract insects, but holds nectar which attracts the bees and aids in pollination. The ghost plant bears one white flower per stem, which blooms for one week only before it fades away and turns black.

The ghost plant reminds you of those who show up in your life like phantom spirits – without warning. You cannot see them approaching, for rather than appearing on your doorstep like everyone else, they pass through the windows and walls of your life, with their translucent, flowy shapes, shattering and disrespecting your boundaries as they enter. You may hear sounds advancing toward you in the distance and believe these to be the tinkling of garden chimes, not knowing that it is the clanging of metal chains of dread and doom that your ghosts are dragging behind them. You will be unprepared for the arrival of your ghosts and unequipped to handle their stay.

Ghosts come at times when you are desperately in need of the give and take of life – when your brilliance has faded and the walls that once surrounded you with protection have begun to crumble and weaken. These phantom people will initially provide something that you believe will aid in your bloom-ing and your survival. But what they really bring is deep and dark and dangerous. And with irresistible and overpowering energy, they will stir up the solid ground in which you are firmly planted. Things inside you that were once deeply rooted will be ripped from their planting place. Parts of you that you have forgotten existed will be churned up. And a powerful whirlwind will blow through you, at once causing chaos and reconnecting you with passions that have been buried, lost, or forgotten.

Life has a way of wearing you down. Lessons learned make you wiser, but they also dull your shiny skin and wear down your bones. Every difficulty you endure moves you further away from the innocent, wide-eyed nymph that once played joyfully among your favorite trees and danced in crisp, autumn leaves until the sun leaked its last light and fell asleep below the treetops. Connecting to your lost innocence, your lost joy, and your lost light is necessary if you want to live life from a place of passion and purpose.

Ghosts can help you connect. You will enter a symbiotic relationship with them. They will give to you. Perhaps what they give isn't decent or true or solid. But it may be exactly what you need at the time. You will give to them. Perhaps what you give is [isn't?] decent and true and solid. But it may be exactly what you need to give at the time.

Ghosts may shower you with painful lessons. But they also allow you to dig deep within yourself and truly love yourself more. You may believe that you can survive without the help of another. Ghosts help you to see that you cannot do life from a place of isolation. You need the stirring of your soul to stay alive. And you need a whole-hearted and loving friendship with yourself to carry on.

When you have reclaimed your wildflower gifts and are embracing the glory and the sacredness of living, you are ready to bid farewell to your ghost – but you will never forget them. You will be amazed that something so vaporous could leave you in possession of such solid offerings. You will be shocked that something you could not hold onto could carve indelible markings deep inside your heart.

You will never forget your ghosts or the valuable things you have learned from them. But with your newfound wisdom and strength, you will have the insight and the courage to say goodbye to your ghosts and release them from your life. You have been haunted long enough.

Fragrance and Memories

"We were together. I forget the rest."
~ Walt Whitman

The scent of a flower is used as a means of advertising to particular insects – letting them know that they possess luscious nectar to feast upon and powdery pollen within its walls. The flying visitors take a golden-pollen dust bath and then deposit remnants of it when they travel to other blooms, causing cross-pollination. Fragrance may also be a way that flowers deter certain herbivores from coming near and munching on their tasty petals – thus their scent aids in their survival. Certain scents attract insects with particular traits that would make them suitable mates and therefore sets the stage for bug love to flourish, with the blossoming of nature's beauty. In this way, flower fragrance serves as an insect matchmaker.

It has been proven that there is a strong link between fragrance and memory. Certain smells attached to specific memories have been seared into your mind. Powerful emotions can be evoked when you catch the scent of a particular flower on the breeze. Emotional memories are stored in the brain. The feelings attached to those memories become stirred up when they are triggered by a particular scent. Emotions come crashing over you like a powerful ocean wave, transporting you to a particular moment in time, one that was perhaps dormant in your mind – buried deep in your past and long forgotten. In this way, fragrance can act as a sort of time machine.

Scents of flowers have also been proven to affect your mood. Lilacs may have a calming effect. Jasmine is known for aiding in relaxation and a few drops of its oil on your pillow may aid better sleep. Rosemary can stimulate memory. Sandalwood can quiet your mind. Peppermint boosts mental clarity. The smell of fresh cut grass may remind you of childhood summers spent endlessly playing outside, without a care in the world. The sweet smell of red roses may remind you of the rose bushes that bloomed in the backyard of your youth. Fragrance is a gateway to cherished memories, along with the emotion associated with them.

Your life consists of moments and memories. The fragrance of your most favorite blooms fades according to climate and time of day. Like the fragrance of beautiful blooms that fade with different conditions, so too do your memories fade. The ones you cherish and cling to throughout your days will be lovingly pressed and stored in your soul. Memories fade due to the natural progression of the passing of years. Other times, our loved ones are afflicted with an illness that robs them of the ability to recall their most cherished moments. This is devastating to witness, wreaking havoc on the person suffering memory loss and leaving loved ones in a helpless state of perpetual grief.

Nothing can erase or steal the love shared between souls. Beautiful relationships are manifestations of love and love doesn't fade like the fragrance of flowers or memories. Love lives on in the hearts and souls of those who experienced it. Allow the shining, miraculous moments of your life to linger by revisiting them where they reside, lovingly tucked away in the chambers of your heart. Face the painful, lesson-laden, pummeling moments by opening yourself up to the present moment. Keep what you learned from your experiences, but don't dwell on tragedy or turmoil. When you embrace today, the fragrance of your one beautiful and wild life swells, leaving no room for the mistakes of yesterday, only for the living and forgiving of today.

When memories fade, relationships blur, and the recognition of who you are to someone slowly begins to disappear, cling tightly to your faith and know that blessed connection cannot be severed. They are born of love, nurtured by moments shared, bathed in the heaven-scented fragrance of angels, and seared into your soul. Love doesn't fade like the memory.

Wild Grass Time

*"Time is too slow fror those who wait, too swift for those who
fear, too long for those who grieve, too short for those who
rejoice, but for those who love, time is eternity."*
~ Henry Van Dyke

*American beach grass is a perennial that grows on sand dunes.
It is an invasive plant that spreads rapidly and thrives under
conditions of high wind and can survive despite being buried
beneath sand. Beach grass grows in tufts along sandy coasts
and reminds us that time moves swiftly in the summer months.*

You always think you have more time. There is supposed to
be more time. Wasn't it just yesterday you were sitting by the
seaside, on a white, sandy beach with the wild grass blowing
in the breeze, listening to the sound of hungry seagulls, the
crashing waves, mixed in with the faint shout of the approaching ice-cream vendor while your skin drank in golden rays of

sunshine and you dreamt of your future? The "mad love" you'd share with someone. Your wedding day – complete with a gorgeous, sparkly gown you'd wear as you floated down the church aisle. The beautiful, precious cherub-like children you'd have. The charming dream house you'd decorate, nestle into, and fill with family. The wild dreams you'd chase and catch and live out under a brilliant, magical star-planted sky, by night, and the sunshine bouncing off colorful flowers that would line the perimeter of your home and climb the white picket fence of your dream life, by day.

Armed with the love of a thousand lifetimes, you'd shelter those you hold close. You'd give your heart, your time, and every fiber of your being to those you move through the world with. You'd help out your parents and attempt to repay them for all they gave you.

There was supposed to be more time. More time before you lost one of them or both of them to the pearly gates of heaven or diseases that robbed their health and memory. And you know in your heart of hearts that you will have great difficulty carrying on without them. Mom, who made you feel loved. Dad, who made you feel safe.

There was supposed to be more time. More time before your siblings lost bits of those deep, everyday connections that kept you entwined and in touch. More time before you grew apart from the forever friends who krew your childhood secrets. More time before the babies you held and rocked ard fed and wrapped around your heart grew bigger and learned to crawl and walk and run and drive and went away to college and moved out far from that childhood dream you used to dream - sitting by the seaside, on a white sandy beach with the wild grass blowing in the breeze.

There was supposed to be more time.

Time is swift and precious. And there is never, ever enough of it. Whatever you want for your life... find it. Find it now, before the wild grass is gone.

Searching for Wildflowers

I'm digging in

Searching through rich, musty soil with
well-polished fingers.
Searching through rocky, jagged pieces that pierce flesh,
draw blood, wound.
Finding the dark places inside me where you grew roots.
What blossomed was unhealthy: Wanting to please.
Working for love. Needing to fix.

I'm digging out.

I'm letting you go. Your brokenness was beautiful. The
pain I felt, exquisite. It taught me. It gave me gifts.
It transformed me.
How powerful I felt trying to save you.
Standing in silhouette, on top of the

world with my garden tools.

Digging the earth.

Turning the soil.

Chopping up roots of hatred into oblivion.

Trying to turn barren hearts into loving ones.

Looking at the world through my wild
rose-colored glasses.

Wanting, needing everyone to see things as I did.

I'm digging in.

I surrender. I lay down my garden tools.

How was I to know they were really weapons?

How was I to know the battle I fought was
against myself?

I'm digging out.

Searching sacred places inside me for glorious things
aching to be released.

Turning my face toward rays of golden sunshine.

I feel warmer. I feel lighter. I feel happier.

I feel whole.

Running through a field of wildflowers

Marveling at their untamed beauty.

Breathing in their courage, their secrets, their strength
to grow – against all odds.

Vibrant colors burst through soil, petals dancing
with delight.

Blue, yellow, red, pink, purple, and orange...
the colors that lived inside me all along.

I'm digging out.

Wishes and Weeds

There are many kinds of wildflowers – and two kinds of people:

Those who see wildflowers as decorating the earth with untamed beauty and bursts of spectacular color. Those who recognize wildflowers as a source of delight. Those who pick them lovingly, to tie with ribbon, arrange into bouquets, or weave into a child's hair.

And those who view wildflowers only as weeds, intruders to be mowed down, sprayed with deadly chemicals, ripped up, and removed from the roots like so much rubbish at the dump.

All of us can learn so much from these wild blossoms. Their very presence asks you to decide what you per-

ceive as beautiful or ugly, what you deem precious or peril-
ous, and what you will choose to toss or keep, hate or love.

In order to find your beauty, your depth, and your gifts, you
must dig deep. And when you do, you may find things
inside you that act as weeds – overpowering and overgrowing the good things that struggle to blossom and beg
to be shared. If you haven't yet fallen in love with yourself
and don't yet believe in your worthiness, these weeds
will threaten your internal wildflowers. They will block the
light that inspires, steal the nourishment that sustains, and
sabotage the love that nurtures your gifts.

But do the work of healing your hurts and forgiving yourself, and the weeds will not win. In fact, you may find that
you feel worthy of your place among the wildflowers.

Weeds are not only internal; you will also most certainly encounter people whose invasive nature stifles your wildflowers. Perhaps you'll be attracted to their uniqueness, cha-
risma, or mystique. Be aware – and beware – of those who
encroach upon your sacred space without your permission,
and weed your life of toxic people whose motives for being
close to you are unclear or unkind. In this way, you'll come
to know your own power.

154

Value and treasure not only what you see with your eyes, but what you feel and know in your heart. When you search for beauty within others, you will find just that. You don't have to love every aspect of a person to honor their worth, but know that it is noble to revere life and see God's reflection everywhere. It takes courage to turn over the soil, dig deep, search for hidden treasure, and risk feeling enormous pain in an effort to love and share yourself with others.

You are here on this earth to help, not just those you understand, but those you are uncomfortable and fearful of helping.

You are here to give, not just what is reasonable to give, but what is unfathomable and impossible to give.

You are here to love, not just the lovable, but those who are broken and difficult to love – which is to say, all of us.

You are here to find your inner wildflowers – the parts of you that remain unspoiled and pure, the parts of you that withstood the world's attempt to erase your uniqueness, the parts of you that remain intact and glorious.

Wildflowers are givers, providing nourishment for birds and

insects. They give without expectation of anything in return and are true survivors. They exist without intervention or help from humans.

But true survival cannot be accomplished without the help of heaven – and therein lies their secret. Look to wildflowers – their characteristics, colors, growth patterns, and return to the soil after their time is through – for clues and insights into how to move through your own life. Grab hold of every bit of the miracle of living. Let nothing stop you from finding your wildflowers, your gifts, the precious things that make you...you.

Don't allow the uncertainty of life to make you fearful and stifle the glorious wildflowers that are aching to burst forth from within. Going through the motions is not living – only existing. Allow yourself to be totally and utterly shaken awake! Once you do, once you've found your brilliant colors, once you've unearthed the sweet fragrance you possess – turn your face toward the golden sunlight. Absorb its nourishment and share your beautiful bounty with the world.

Live Like a Wildflower

Grow outside of fences. Grow against all odds.

Grow through cracks in concrete. Grow in ways no one

ever believed you could.

Be tough. Be tender. Be wild.

Dig deep.

Find the gifts inside you aching to be released.

The ones only you possess.

The ones the world desperately needs in order to heal.

Sharing them offers those you meet on your journey

permission to do the same.

Celebrate your imperfections.

The ones you hide because you believe they make you

unlovable. They are your glorious trademarks

and they distinguish you as a miracle.

Be brave. Be strong. Be fierce.

Search for the million sacred reasons
why your soul was planted here.
Learn your lessons.
But don't allow yourself to be used, ripped from the
ground, and discarded.
When they call you a common weed, show them your
billowy, white puffy seeds and let the breeze
carry you away.
Surround yourself near those capable of seeing your
unmatched beauty and wish upon it.
Risk everything for love.
Love with wild abandon, even if you are left broken,
shattered, and lost.
Let all the phases of your life meld as you
paint with bold, deliberate strokes
the life you are meant to live.
Use the most vibrant wildflower colors that live inside
you and beg to be set free.
Recognize the etched faces inside your painting.
Those you have loved and lost and held close and
pushed away and still miss with every blessed breath
that reaches your lungs and every precious bit of love

that reaches your heart.
Let the earth rejoice because YOU are here.
And with naked, dusty, summer feet, walk and
dance and stumble through all the cool, rugged
pathways of your journey,
until you find your direction, your stride,
your place of belonging.
Watch as the brilliant star-planted sky twinkles, like
a magical light show from concerts of your youth.
And before the last star is extinguished and your
meadow goes dark, let the soft, spirited winds
deliver a message from your Maker that you have
been yearning to hear forever...

WELCOME HOME, WILDFLOWER.

Acknowledgements

With Love and gratitude…

Thank you to my husband, Mark and my sons, Mark and Nick. You are the sweetest part of my life, and nothing compares to the feeling of pure joy I experience when I am in your presence. I love you more.

Thank you to my mom, Rose, for being a model of strength, grace and beauty, for teaching me to see the goodness in others, and for making me feel loved and special always. The memories you have lost, live on in the deepest parts of my heart, and they help sustain me…through it all.

Thank you to my dad, Frank, for being my greatest teacher. During the writing of this book, I heard your voice in my head, saying, "Carole, how do you come up with all this stuff?" And when I drew the illustrations, it was your hand that guided me. I miss you.

Thank you to Maria, Evie, Sharon, Rosann, Frank, and Jim for being there since the beginning. Nothing that life throws our way, can ever break our bond or diminish our love.

Thank you to Jena Schwartz for the gentle care and editing that you gave to "my baby". Thank you to Jessie Vezza for your talents in helping to create the design of this book. Thank you to all my family members and all my friends for your love and support. The connections I share with you…make me love life more.

Resources

Sanders, Joseph. **The Secrets of Wildflowers**: A Delightful Feast of Little-Known Facts, Folklore, and History. Connecticut: Lyons Press, 2003

Gibbons, Bob. **Wildflower Wonders**: The 50 Best Wildflower Sites in the World. Princeton and Oxford: Princeton University Press, 2011

Houk, Rose. **Eastern Wildflowers: A Photographic Celebration from New England to the Heartland**. San Francisco: Chronicle Books, 1950

Burger, William C. **Flowers: How they Changed the World**. Amherst, New York: Prometheus Books, 2006

Chace, Teri Dunn. **Seeing Flowers: Discover the Hidden Life of Flowers**. Portland and London: Timber Press, 2013

Newcomb, Lawrence. **Newcomb's Wildflower Guide**. New York, Boston, and London: Little, Brown and Company, 1977

First Printing 2017

Harvest Moon Publishing
ISBN-13 978 -0692810132
ISBN-10 0692810137

Author's Website: www.carolerosedowhan.com

Author photograph by deborahannphotography
Cover photo and illustations by Carole Rose Dowhan